P9-AGP-003

BOOKS BY JAMES BALDWIN

Go Tell It on the Mountain

Notes of a Native Son

Giovanni's Room

Nobody Knows My Name

Another Country

The Fire Next Time

Nothing Personal (with Richard Avedon)

Blues for Mister Charlie

Going to Meet the Man

Tell Me How Long the Train's Been Gone

The Amen Corner

A Rap on Race (with Margaret Mead)

No Name in the Street

A Dialogue (with Nikki Giovanni)

One Day, When I Was Lost

If Beale Street Could Talk

The Devil Finds Work

Little Man, Little Man: A Story of Childhood
(with Yoran Cazac)

The Story of Siegfried

THE
EVIDENCE OF
THINGS NOT SEEN

THE
EVIDENCE OF
THINGS NOT SEEN

Reissued Edition

JAMES BALDWIN

A HOLT PAPERBACK

HENRY HOLT AND COMPANY

NEW YORK

Holt Paperbacks
Henry Holt and Company
Publishers since 1866
120 Broadway
New York, New York 10271
www.henryholt.com

A Holt Paperback® and Ⓗ® are registered trademarks of
Macmillan Publishing Group, LLC.

Copyright © 1985 by James Baldwin and 1995 by the James Baldwin Estate
Foreword from the Ten-Year Anniversary Edition copyright © 1995
by Derrick Bell and Janet Dewart Bell
Foreword copyright © 2023 by Stacey Abrams
All rights reserved.
Distributed in Canada by Raincoast Book Distribution Limited

Library of Congress Cataloging-in-Publication Data

Names: Baldwin, James, 1924–1987, author.
Title: The evidence of things not seen / James Baldwin.
Description: Reissued edition. | New York, NY : Holt Paperbacks, [2023] |
  "Originally published in hardcover in 1985 by Holt, Rinehart and
  Winston"—Verso.
Identifiers: LCCN 2022041761 (print) | LCCN 2022041762 (ebook) |
  ISBN 9781250844897 (trade paperback) | ISBN 9781250886729 (ebook)
Subjects: LCSH: Williams, Wayne Bertram. | Serial murders—
  Georgia—Atlanta—Case studies. | Racism—Georgia—Atlanta. |
  Atlanta (Ga.)—Race relations.
Classification: LCC HV6534.A7 B35 2023 (print) | LCC HV6534.A7 (ebook) |
  DDC 364.152/3209758231—dc23/eng/20221021
LC record available at https://lccn.loc.gov/2022041761
LC ebook record available at https://lccn.loc.gov/2022041762

Our books may be purchased in bulk for promotional, educational, or business
use. Please contact your local bookseller or the Macmillan Corporate and
Premium Sales Department at (800) 221-7945, extension 5442, or by e-mail at
MacmillanSpecialMarkets@macmillan.com.

Originally published in hardcover in 1985 by Holt, Rinehart and Winston

First Holt Paperbacks Edition 2023

Designed by Meryl Sussman Levavi

Printed in the United States of America

3   5   7   9   10   8   6   4

For David Baldwin, the father and the son

Faith is the substance of things hoped for, the evidence of things not seen.

—St. Paul

A dog starv'd at his master's gate
Predicts the ruin of the state.

—William Blake

FOREWORD

"Joan Crawford's straight, narrow, and lonely back." My first encounter with James Baldwin occurred in this opening line of *The Devil Finds Work*. More than thirty years on, I remember that terse opening with perfect clarity—the introduction to a memoir that served as a fitting gateway to the intricacies of his mind, to his nimble, rancorous explorations of the inherent contradictions in our lived experiences. Since then, Baldwin's books have become a steady fixture in my reading habits, augmented by his caustic, honest television interviews and his wide-ranging commentaries.

First published by Baldwin nearly forty years ago, *The Evidence of Things Not Seen* offers a searing disquisition on race, class, identity, and community, not unfamiliar territory to him but uniquely approached. Framed as a journeyman's investigation of the Atlanta child murders from 1979 to 1981, Baldwin's work explores how privilege sacrifices the young and vulnerable, especially black children, denying them voice and possibly vengeance. His masterful rendering of a complex case that did not pretend to have an answer—even at the time it went to trial—continues to prod the conscience. In fact, Atlanta's mayor, Keisha Lance Bottoms, ordered a reexamination of the case in 2021, and investigators have raised questions about the number of victims claimed during the murderous spell.

Forty years ago, the tumult that surrounded the vile killings of Atlanta's black children tangled notions of guilt and accountability, reality and sharp relief, which remain snarled in both the public imagination and in the vagaries of what constitutes justice. But, at the core of his incisive writing, Baldwin issues a weary, pointed challenge to the reader, asking if we are ever truly in search of the truth, decades on. At the core of his analysis is our duty of care for the lives of black folks. Atlanta, Georgia's legendary status as a mecca for black wealth, talent, and political acumen tacitly argues that this obligation should have no better keepers. Yet, Baldwin juxtaposes this mythology with the spectacle of Wayne Williams's murder trial for the slaying of two men, as proxy for the killings of more than two dozen black children.

I cannot claim to know the Atlanta Baldwin encountered during his visit in 1985; although I have claimed Georgia as my home since 1989, and I eventually worked with or for some of the folks included in his commentary. Born in Wisconsin, and raised in Mississippi, I moved to Decatur, Georgia, in the autumn with my parents and five siblings. By then, the specter of the serial killings had long since faded from headlines. When the Williams trial began in 1982, I had just reached the age of eight, the same age as some of the youngest victims; and with the safety of two states' distance, I was blithely unaware of the stark, relentless terror that had gripped the black families of Atlanta in my early youth.

Nevertheless, Baldwin's account of the social peril, the discord between power and poverty, the tenor of the investigation and trial immediately thrusts the reader into a cultural maelstrom, audited by his distance as an interloper and raconteur. He cites familiar tropes about the African-American enclaves that comprise Atlanta, and his fluency anchors us in the Southern dichotomy that birthed Atlanta mayor Maynard Jackson, Wayne Williams, and the KKK. Baldwin effectively guides the uninitiated through the stoic grief of the slain victims' families, urging us to recall how the anguish of black parents can be too easily overlooked. With pointed genius, he inveighs against the comfortable dismissal of the broken policies that allowed nearly thirty children to perish.

The Evidence of Things Not Seen channels the cri de coeur of the slain and their beloveds and pours their indignation into the twenty-first century. Baldwin's indictment of how economic paucity and race can doom us echoes, as it must, with the murders of George Floyd, Breonna Taylor, and Ahmaud Arbery in 2020. Millions have watched the endless replays of Floyd's public execution by a dismissive police officer who knelt on his neck until his breath choked away. While the catharsis of trial put Derek Chauvin into a prisoner's cell, the antidote to this brutality remains mired in legislative limbo. The U.S. Congress, no longer hostage to national protests, has abandoned its pledge of "never again" despite the regular stories of law enforcement misdeeds. Baldwin's cautions in *The Evidence of Things Not Seen* warn us of the difference between individuals and systems—a difference that demands we judge officers of the law fairly by their actions but requires that we indict the impermeable protections of qualified immunity, racial profiling, and violent policing practices like choke holds.

The murder of Breonna Taylor, while she nestled in her bed, came at the hands of Louisville, Kentucky, law enforcement that randomly fired rounds of ammunition into her home after failing to give Breonna a chance to offer a token defense. This horrific miscarriage of policing power animated her mother, Tamika Palmer. Ms. Palmer's crusade—like Camille Bell's demand back then that Atlanta leaders protect black children despite their failure to protect her own—is the legacy of what Baldwin exhorts of those who read his reportage. Our systems place unfair burdens on victims' families to bring righteousness to the process—regardless of the color of the bad actor. Just as Bell decried inaction, Palmer forced changes to no-knock warrants and trained a fine eye on a fumbling state attorney general whose blackness could not be used to excuse his flawed leadership on Breonna Taylor's case.

Closer to home, in Brunswick, Georgia, the vigilante murder of Ahmaud Arbery implicated a district attorney who refused to indict the killers or truly mount an investigation. Two white men chased jogger Ahmaud through the streets of town on suspicion of being too black for the neighborhood. Their cavalier shootings—captured on video—nearly went unattended. Black families in Brunswick, Georgia, refused to be ignored by political leaders and banded together to demand action. As of this writing, the state's murder case resulted in a guilty verdict against all three defendants, but the federal hate crimes charges are still wending their way through the courts. The consequences have been more telling than Baldwin might have presaged: the murderers convicted in a trial of peers, the disgraced district attorney deposed and under indictment, and the repeal of Georgia's citizen's arrest law. That particularly depraved statute received initial codification in Georgia in 1863 to aid in the enforcement of slavery—when black skin meant chattel property, not humanity.

The humanity of black children, of black men and women, of black lives, has ever been a conundrum for America. Forty years on, Baldwin's writing reminds us that we have never resolved the core query: Do black lives matter? Unequivocally, the moral answer is yes, but James Baldwin refuses such rhetorical comfort. The persistence of mass incarceration, criminal injustice, voter suppression, environmental racism, COVID disparities, and the host of ills that inevitably gain stronger purchase in black communities begs the question be given more urgent action. Whether the proof is introduced in trials, in the streets, or in the halls of power, we are devoid as a nation until we answer with a single voice. Until then, we continue to grapple with the evidence of things not seen.

—STACEY Y. ABRAMS

PREFACE

Walter Lowe, of *Playboy*, wrote me—to my home in France—suggesting that I go to Atlanta to do a story concerning the missing and (as it evolved) murdered children. I had been following the story—what there was, that is, in the foreign press, to follow. It is not so easy to follow a story occurring in one's own country from the vantage point of another one.

From afar, one may imagine that one perceives the pattern. And one may. But, as one is not challenged—or, more precisely, menaced—by the details, the pattern may be nothing more than something one imagines oneself to be able to remember.

And, after all, what I remembered—or imagined myself to remember—of my life in America (before I left home!) was terror. And what I am trying to suggest by what *one imagines oneself to be able to remember* is that terror cannot be remembered. One blots it out. The organism—the human being—blots it out.

One invents, or creates, a personality or a *persona*. Beneath this accumulation (rock of ages!) sleeps or hopes to sleep, that terror which the memory repudiates.

Yet, it never sleeps—that terror, which is not the terror of death (which cannot be imagined) but the terror of being destroyed.

Sometimes I think, one child in Atlanta said to me, *that I'll be coming home from* (baseball or football) *practice and somebody's car will come behind me and I'll be thrown into the trunk of the car and it will be dark and he'll drive the car away and I'll never be found again.*

Never be found again: that terror is far more vivid than the fear of death. When the child said that to me I tried to imagine the tom-tom silence of the trunk of the car, the darkness, the silence, the speed, the corkscrew road. I tried, that is, to imagine this as something happening to the child. My memory refused to accommodate that child as myself.

But that child *was* myself.

I do not remember, will never remember, how I howled and screamed the first time my mother was carried away from me. My mother was the only human being in the world. The *only* human being: everyone else existed by her permission.

Yet, what the memory repudiates controls the human being. What one does not remember dictates who one loves or fails to love. What one does not remember dictates, actually, whether one plays poker, pool, or chess. What one does not remember contains the key to one's tantrums or one's poise. What one does not remember is the serpent in the garden of one's dreams. What one does not remember is the key to one's performance in the toilet or in bed. What one does not remember contains the only hope, danger, trap, inexorability, of love—only love can help you recognize what you do not remember.

And memory makes its only real appearance in this life as this life is ending—appearing, at last, as a kind of guide into a condition which is as far beyond memory as it is beyond imagination.

What has this to do with the murdered, missing children of Atlanta?

It has something to do with the fact that no one wishes to be plunged, head down, into the torrent of what he does not remember and does not wish to remember. It has something to do with the fact that we all came here as candidates for the slaughter of the innocents. It has something to do with the fact that all survivors, however they accommodate or fail to remember it, bear the inexorable guilt of the survivor. It has something to do, in my own case, with having once been a Black child in a White country.

My memory stammers: but my soul is a witness.

THE CASE AGAINST Wayne Williams contains a hole so wide that the indisputably alert Abby Mann has driven one of his many tanks through it. To discuss his docudrama demands another essay entirely—involving the American sense of history, for example, or Commerce, the evil grown by the tree of the doctrine of White Supremacy and the Tree of Manifest Destiny, and the many shapes collusion or collaboration take. His docudrama, furthermore, and by no means incidentally, demands the services of many people for whom I have the greatest respect.

I will merely point out, and beg my reader to remember,

that his portraits of the Mayor, and the Chief of Police, are, to put it with the utmost restraint, irresponsibly wide of the mark and that the role of the White cop is a necessary American invention.

On the other hand, the scene in which the boy calls the Task Force, which did not arrive, *is* true: this story was told to me by one of the children. Ms. Bell *and* Ms. Foster, who portrays her, are more complex than the docudrama can imagine or convey. The real meaning of the boiler explosion at the housing project is not conveyed—for the reason that the docudrama is too self-serving to be able to convey the reality of that moment in Atlanta.

Georgia is named for an English King and enters History as a convict colony: which is to say that the people who *settled* Georgia had no choice but to become *White* there.

This is one of the keys to that monumentally self-serving fable, *Gone with the Wind*, and to Scarlett O'Hara's two most revealing lines: *As God is my witness, I'll never go hungry again*, and, over and over, *I can't think about that now, I'll go crazy if I do—I'll think about that tomorrow!*

History, I contend, is the present—*we*, with every breath we take, every move we make, *are* History—and what goes around, comes around.

—JAMES BALDWIN
April 2, 1985
Atlanta, New York, Amherst, St. Paul de Vence

THE
EVIDENCE OF
THINGS NOT SEEN

I~T WAS NEVER SAID, IN SO MANY WORDS, BUT EVERYONE appeared to suspect that this particular computer had had its own reasons for selecting this particular judge.

Each of us knows, though we do not like this knowledge, that a courtroom is a visceral Roman circus. No one involved in this contest is, or can be, impartial. One makes the attempt, or imagines that one does: but it is, in any case, and strenuously, an attempt. Or, in other words, the ability to suspend judgment is, in each of us, suspect—to leave it at that: without, that is, going so far as to say that the suspension of judgment is impossible.

For to suspend judgment demands that one dismiss one's perceptions at the very same moment that one is most crucially—and cruelly—dependent on them. We perceive by means of the kaleidoscopic mirror of this life. This means that our ability to perceive is at once tyrannized by our expectations, and at war with them. Our expectations are revealed in our habits, our manner: our defeats, terrors, genuine or imagined triumphs risk being more visible to others than to ourselves: for that *mirror, mirror, on the wall!* hears no questions and answers none.

The light is always changing in that mirror. This light will not permit us to forget that we are mortal: which means that we are all connected—which complicates the judgment.

It is one thing to be part of the audience at the courtroom Roman circus, and quite another matter to be in the ring. The audience is there to distract or justify itself with questions of right or wrong. The gladiators know only that one of them must win. They are not suspending judgment. They are *creating* judgment: ours.

The circus and the audience are absolutely indispensable to the hygiene of the State.

The judge that the computer selected is a young and very likable Black man, Clarence Cooper. He is one of the many Black legal talents nurtured by District Attorney Lewis Slaton. Slaton is a White native Atlantan, and he guided the Prosecution—although, according to some of the people I met, "guided" is not the word.

Judge Cooper, the younger of two children, was born on May 5, 1942, in Decatur, Georgia. Decatur is a suburb of Atlanta. But, a "suburb" of Atlanta in 1942 is not at all the same entity as a suburb of Atlanta in 1982: which may be why Cooper was raised in Cincinnati. His birthplace is, in any case, ambiguous. It means that he can or cannot claim, as do so many others, *I'm from Atlanta. I'm not from Georgia.*

This claim struck me as a stubborn and stunning delusion. It is as though I should claim, for example, that *I'm from*

Harlem. I'm not from New York. The intention, or the meaning, of the claim is clear; but Harlem is not an independent entity or nation. It exists in, and is controlled by, the city and state of New York. Or, if, on another level I should proclaim, in Europe—or in Africa—to be from New York but not from America, one would be justified in worrying about my sanity, to say nothing of my reliability. I do not mean to go so far, as concerns my friends in Atlanta, but this has been their posture since we first met—in 1957—and may be one of the keys, if keys there are, to the city.

Atlanta is a railroad town, comes into existence, that is, around one of the triumphs of the Industrial Revolution—the railroad—and it was first called, bleakly enough, Terminus. This was in the 1830s, when the institution of slavery had a few more years left in it than does the present century. It is inland, which is why General Sherman had to march to the sea, destroying a crucial segment of the Confederacy's transportation system. "He didn't destroy great works of art, or the opera, because they weren't here—there was *nothing* here." There was, probably, a little more than "nothing," but Atlanta's eminence was and is as a commercial hub, a wheeling-and-dealing transportation center, and one of the world's busiest and most interminable airports has taken the place of the railroads.

But Atlanta's high visibility and commercial importance do not mean that Atlanta is not in the state of Georgia. This is one of the reasons—the principal reason—that, during the plague years of the child murders, and, then, the arrest, and, then, the trial, Atlanta's leitmotif was the presence, and responsibility, of the Black Administration. The presence of a Black Administration—as distinguished, perhaps, from an incontestable actuality—proved that the "city too busy to hate" could not be accused of administering "Southern" justice. (It proved nothing of the sort, not only because Atlanta belongs to the state of Georgia but because Georgia belongs to the United States.)

Cooper's mother was a maid and his father drove a truck. His father was disabled in 1966, when Cooper would have been twenty-four. He was twenty-one at the moment of the March on Washington, in 1963, and the same age when Medgar Evers was assassinated, earlier that same year, and when Kennedy, the only president to whom he could have felt any allegiance, was murdered, twenty-two when Malcolm was murdered, and twenty-five when Martin was blown away.

I met the Judge only once, hence cannot claim to know the man. His major, in Clark College, in 1964, was political science and history. He was twenty-two then, and forty when I met him—as a judge—which suggests a swift and strong-willed passage on a rocky road.

In June 1981, after twenty-two months and twenty-eight corpses, Wayne Bertram Williams, then twenty-three, was arrested for murder. That he is Black is important, since the Administration of the city is Black, and all of the murdered children were Black.

It is also important that he was not charged with twenty-eight murders, but with two: the last two, those of Jimmy Ray Payne and Nathaniel Cater.

These last two, however, were not children, but grown men—no matter how alcoholic or "retarded" they may have been: and, anyway, at the bottom level of poverty and despair it is hard to judge who is "retarded." I was told that, because they were "retarded," they were *perceived* as children: I found this unconvincing. Though, as I was abruptly forced to realize,

I had not the faintest notion as to what impelled a man to murder children, it yet seemed to me—hopefully, perhaps—that this impulse had to be special. A man who murdered children was not likely to perceive a male adult as a male child. This meant, though, that I was approaching the quicksand of my ignorance and judgment had to be suspended.

Atlanta's reaction to the arrest and trial of Wayne Williams (as distinguished from the national reaction, insofar as there was any) suggests both the bitter and bewildered apathy that succeeds exhaustion and the instinctive attempt to calculate the meaning of the new dimension suddenly given to an old dilemma. Runaway children are nothing new, nor is the slaughtered Black man-child. Children become unruly, they roam the streets, they run away—that's one thing: boys will be boys. (Though two of the murdered children were girls, which would seem, to me, to violate the "pattern" that Slaton claims proves the guilt of Wayne Williams.) But, then, instead of the phone call or the letter or the telegram or the visit to the precinct or the visit to the hospital, or, even, to the morgue, the missing children begin turning up, dead—in the weeds, by the roadside, in abandoned sites, in the river. It is very clear that whoever is murdering the children *wants* them to be found as they are found: this brutally indifferent treatment of the child's corpse is like spitting in the faces of the people who produced the child.

The imagination is poorly equipped to accommodate an action in which one, instinctively, recognizes the orgasmic release of self-hatred.

The imagination is poorly equipped to deal with this action because self-hatred is so common, and takes so many forms: it is not a local or a racial or a regional matter. In the present case, given the bottom-line realities of life in these so ambiguously United States, the missing, menaced, murdered children were menaced by color and locality: they were—visibly—Black, which, in this Republic, is a kind of doom, and actually poor—which condition elicits from the land of opportunity and the work ethic a judgment as merciless as it is defensive.

The South, however, and the nation, are full of people who *look* White and *are* Black: some claim their ancestry and some seal it off with a change of address, nor are their new neighbors likely to challenge their identity, being so uncertain of their own. In the United States, as in South Africa, one's color is a matter of the legal definition, and/or experience, and/or, finally, choice.

The Colored, of South Africa, for example, are—or were—a legal creation: *half-breeds*, or *mulattoes*, to use the elegant and civilized terms of the Civilized—people pale enough to hope to be treated as White. Or, surrendering the hope of an earthly paradise, at least not to be treated as Black. This aspiration, during their purgatory—so it was hoped and intended—would cause them to ally themselves with White Power instead of Black insurrection. This policy failed when the Colored, flying in the face of Law and Order, and repudiating the definitions of the State, declared themselves—quite illegally—to be Black.

And, in this country, someone who looks White and who, refusing to deny his Black ancestry, declares himself Black, has made a genuine and, sometimes, a genuinely moral choice. (I state the matter in this somewhat tentative way because the choice, especially given the choices this country offers, can sometimes be merely expedient or political.)

In any case, this country, in toto, from Atlanta to Boston, to Texas, to California, is not so much a vicious racial caldron—

many, if not most countries, are that—as a paranoid color wheel. Some people would like to step out of their White skins and some people loathe their Black skins. Some people hate their White kinfolk and some people fear their Black kinfolk. And, however we confront or fail to confront this most crucial truth concerning our history—American history—everybody pays for it and everybody knows it. The only way *not* to know it is to retreat into the Southern madness indeed, the inability to face this most particular and specific truth *is* the Southern madness. But, as someone told me, long ago, *The spirit of the South is the spirit of America.*

Whoever was murdering the children, then, could, literally, have been anyone, of any color, from the teacher to the preacher to the cop to the bus driver to your neighbor to you: all would, or could, have had the same motive. Underlying the tremendous unwillingness to believe that a Black person could be murdering Black children was the specifically Southern knowledge and experience of how much Black blood is in White veins—and how much White blood is in Black veins.

Thus, it was slowly and reluctantly decided that the murderer had to be someone dark *enough* to pass unnoticed in Black neighborhoods: just as some of one's cousins or brothers or sisters or nieces or nephews had been light enough to pass as White.

Some of the children have been shot, some stabbed, some strangled. Some are naked, some are clothed, some are decomposing.

You don't know all of them, but you know some. The last time you saw this one or that one, he was in the kitchen, with *your* child.

You begin waiting for your child to come home.

Under the best of circumstances, and in the most accommodating of places, it is impossible to keep an adolescent male child at home. And the curfew in the *Casbah*, designed to get Black kids in off the streets before eleven p.m., never had the remotest possibility of being enforced. Boys will be boys indeed, and with a vengeance, and, for many a poor boy the most perceptible difference between the streets and home is that home is danger and squalor with a blanket and a roof. And Mama, sometimes Daddy, and the other kids, and the choking, incoherent, intolerable sense that he must *do* something!

And no young person has ever heard a warning. *Ain't nobody going to mess with me*, he tells you, believing it—of course, all children do—and then he doesn't come home.

I realized, after the first few days in Atlanta, that I choked on, could not ask the general, cheerful, universal question, *How're the kids?* Without realizing it, one sought the answer to the unasked question in the eyes of the man or the woman one was facing.

I was surprised, one person told me, *at the absence of the Black* presence *at the trial. We* just weren't there. It was as though we didn't want to believe that this was happening, that one of us could do this!

Oh, yes, said another, *it means we in the* White *shit, now! They got us. They win—when a Black person can do this!*

The Black man who has been tried for two murders and—for the moment—condemned as the mass murderer of Black children is an odd creature: but so would you or I be, sitting on the witness stand, under such an aura. He is not, literally or legally, *accused* of being a mass murderer: but he is the only suspect, and he is *assumed* to be a mass murderer.

Once under suspicion, and so dreadful a suspicion, everything the person does is intolerably suspect—beginning, perhaps, with his intolerable assumption that he has any right to be born. It is much, much simpler, after all, and more considerate, for the accused to agree, at once, to be guilty. With this agreement, we are released from the ordeal of imposing or suspending judgment. This creature, trapped, at bay, looks toward us as his only hope—and: we *are* his only hope.

Beneath the microscope of the inquisition, everything this creature does—smiling or not smiling, calm or panic-stricken, belching or not belching, sweating or not sweating, smoking or not smoking, shouting or not shouting—is suspect. This is because *he* is suspect, having had no better sense, or better luck, which comes to the same thing, than to force himself on the exasperated public, and sorely tried democratic attention. He wants to leave this place, and go home: and so do the people who have been dragged here, against their will, to sit in judgment on him.

Their task is not simplified by the fact that the case against him is compromised by emotional, moral, and legal confusion.

The city too busy to hate has undergone the ordeal of twenty-eight—the official count—violently publicized murders. Black death has never before elicited so much attention. The attention, the publicity, given to the slaughter becomes, itself, one more aspect of an unforgivable violation. I have dismissed the national reaction because it certainly did not rival the American reaction to the fate of the hostages in Iran—or, for that matter, the raid on Entebbe. No one made vows, or lit candles: it was, eventually, just another TV news spot concerning the trials of a friendly but disastrously underdeveloped area. But some people sold green ribbons, for the children of Atlanta, and money from every description of private citizen came pouring into the city: some to the Mayor's office and some to the Stop the Murders Mothers' Committee, headed by Camille Bell. (We will discuss this very important committee presently. The money issue was to precipitate—though it was not responsible for—some bitterly revealing exchanges.)

Atlanta became, for a season, a kind of grotesque Disneyland. Prophets, soothsayers, mediums, political aspirants, and political ruins all had their say, along with a couple from—I believe—Philadelphia, who raise hunting dogs and had brought some with them and who went out with the search party every day, and some of the young men who, under other circumstances, had taken it upon themselves to be responsible for the safety of New York subway passengers.

There was, of course, in all of this, something humiliating and intolerable, and, as usual, all this grotesque activity submerged, or nearly submerged, more serious efforts made by, for example, Mohammed Ali and Sammy Davis, Jr., and Frank Sinatra *and* Dick Gregory: their bizarre theories did not seem so unspeakable to me. But we will return to this aspect of the Atlanta ordeal. While it was going on a friend of mine described it, with a certain bitterly flippant accuracy, as *buck-dancing on the graves!*

The case against Williams struck me as so dubious that I wondered how and why it had been brought into court. *How* has something to do with the pressure brought to bear by, of all people, the FBI. *Why* has to do with the fact that the commercial viability of the city too busy (making money) to hate was in danger.

The Atlanta air rings and stings of twenty-eight murders. But this is not the first time such a devastation has occurred: it is the first time that Authority has been forced to recognize the devastation as crucial, and, incontestably, it is this resonance that has brought about the trial. But Wayne Williams is not *legally* accused of twenty-eight murders, even though, I repeat, it is the climate created by these murders which has placed him on the witness stand. Wayne Williams is accused—legally—of two murders. But he is assumed to be guilty of twenty-eight murders, and, without being charged with these crimes, is being tried for them. For the Prosecution insists that there is a "pattern" to the murders of the children, which, when Wayne Williams is found guilty of the two, will "link" him to the other twenty-six.

Now, this labyrinthine approach to justice must present itself to the layman—to say nothing of the accused—as a somewhat unprecedented basis for a murder trial. Either the accused is being tried for twenty-eight murders or for two. If he is *not* being tried for twenty-eight murders, it can only be, after all, for lack of evidence. How, then, does it happen—legally—that a man charged with *two* murders can be tried for twenty-eight?

The Prosecution, having, obviously, no option, has based its case on circumstantial evidence. This species of circumstantial evidence (the "fiber" evidence, to be considered) is, itself, unprecedented in the legal history of the United States. Not only is it unprecedented: it is, also, *scientific*. This can be taken to mean that the layman (in this case, the jury), who may or may not be able to understand it, will certainly not be able to understand it well enough to be able to challenge or refute it. And it must be added, too, however one may wish to avoid or deny it, that the history and the situation of Black people in this country amounts to an indictment of America's legal and moral history.

Quite a witch's brew, and the principal actors in this drama are (as far as the naked eye can see) Black. And Williams is either a mass murderer—a fairly rare species, after all, if one dismisses the aspirations of the military—or a kind of Loeb-Leopold basket case, in living color.

One is forced to conclude, then, that Wayne Williams has been arrested, and tried, *because* of twenty-eight murders, and been found guilty of what turns out to be an indeterminate number. No one who was in Atlanta can say that this had the effect of causing Atlanta to sleep more easily. The judgment did not release, but exacerbated an intolerable tension. Camille Bell, for example, turned herself into a one-woman defense committee for the parents of the accused, and, along with almost all the other mothers, repudiates the verdict. Only Ms. Mathis, mother of the sixth victim, Jeffrey Mathis, welcomed the verdict, saying that life was too good for the murderer of her son and that her only regret was that Williams had not been condemned to the electric chair. But Ms. Hill, mother of Timothy Hill, one of the last victims, cries, *"Why, they just done forgot about Timmy!"*

To repeat, then, for this is important, Williams has never been accused, legally, of having committed twenty-eight murders, and he has not been tried for twenty-eight murders. He has been tried and condemned for two murders, and, even for these two the evidence is far from overwhelmingly convincing ("because of an FBI screw-up"; but we will return to the FBI). The nature of the two murders for which he has been condemned does not really call to mind the other twenty-six: it does *not* demand a suspension of judgment to realize that a murdered man is not a murdered child. It is the emotional climate of Atlanta, to say nothing of the power of the State—by which I mean both the state of Georgia and the Republic to which, on the basis of its history and its testimony, Georgia so reluctantly belongs—that creates, permits, this "link." For, without this "link," it is perfectly possible—indeed, it is likely—that the last two murders, of two anonymous drifters, would not have been noticed at all, especially, I must repeat, in the Deep South.

Hence, the connection of the two murders with the previous twenty-six has absolutely no legal validity. No one has been tried for these murders and no one, therefore, can be condemned for them. In the ordinary way of the Law, the People would have been enjoined to concentrate on the two murders and forget about the twenty-six: to study the *legal* accusation of *two* murders, not twenty-eight—but this is not what happened.

The beleaguered and, also, unhappily, divided Defense could scarcely have avoided falling into the trap so carefully laid for them. Their legal obligation was to defend their client against a double murder charge. But the Prosecution had absolutely no interest in this double murder, and it is doubtful, furthermore, that they had a case. Williams was on trial as a mass murderer, which charge, having no legal validity, could find no legal defense.

The Judge, for example, allowed the contestable principle of "prior acts" to be used by the Prosecution against the defendant. "Prior acts" is meant to establish a "pattern." The accused, that is, prior to the events that have caused him to be accused, and having no direct relationship to the accusation, has, nevertheless, been observed to be capable of, or addicted to, certain habits, or styles of behavior. He may, for example, have been observed playing chess, or Monopoly, at midnight, with fourteen-year-old boys—or fourteen-year-old girls—or his mother—or alone. He may have been observed, standing on a street corner, or in an alleyway, or his kitchen or someone else's kitchen, or a bar, or a toilet, talking to a boy or a girl or a man or a cat or a woman or your wife or his sister or himself: there is nothing that won't, under pressure, establish a "pattern," and, once one begins looking for a "pattern," this "pattern" will prove anything you want it to prove.

The reasons Wayne Williams gives, for example, for being on the bridge at around four o'clock in the morning, when he, allegedly, dumped a body into the river, do not make much sense. The Johnson woman, with whom he had an appointment later that same morning, and whose address he was attempting to verify, would appear to exist only in his imagination. In any case, it seems an odd moment to undertake such an errand. As he was not arrested on the bridge and his car was not searched, we really must take as hearsay, after the fact, the nylon cords in the car, and the blood on the seats. (The failure to arrest Wayne Williams, at that moment, became known as "the FBI screw-up.")

I do not know how a murderer sounds, just after disposing of the corpse, or how *I* would sound, explaining my presence on the bridge at that hour of the morning. But I know that I might have had many reasons, all of them, from my own point of view, guilty, or private: these two words being, very often, alas, synonyms among us. I also know that I might not have wished to explain anything at all to the cops. I was certainly like that when I was young and I am not so very different now. In any case, arrogance, loneliness, and youth may or may not indicate the capacity to commit murder, since everyone, in principle, is capable of murder. But this capacity can be recognized (*mirror, mirror, on the wall!*) only after the fact.

Wayne Williams is the only child of Faye and Homer Williams, born long after they had stopped hoping to have any children. He was, thus, as a male, a doubly special child and the only aspect of his life on which there appears to be general agreement is that he was terribly spoiled by his parents.

This would seem, on the whole, to be true, and, however unfortunate, probably inevitable; but it is just as well to bear in mind that the country, to say nothing of the world, is catastrophic with spoiled children and that we would not be discussing this one—would never have heard of him at all—were it not for the circumstances that have forced him on our attention. This fact does not afford us any clue as to whether or not he is capable of murder. The heirs to the throne of England are all, for example, spoiled brats, issue of bloodstained conquerors—which tells us something, but not enough, about the Prince of Wales.

Andrew Young met Wayne Williams, and some of his friends, when Wayne was about twelve or thirteen—"they all looked about twelve," Andy says—when Wayne wanted to interview him for his radio station. Not having the faintest idea of what he was getting himself into, Andy went along. The station turned out to be a community station, operating "illegally"— that is, without a license—out of Wayne's basement. "Some of the most impressive kids I'd ever met" interviewed Andrew Young for about half an hour.

Something in Andy's tone, as he spoke of this encounter, struck me with great force: his tone conveyed his love, and his respect, for the young.

The young are the community's sacred—and only—hope, and it is the responsibility of the elders to guide and protect and raise the young—which means, also, and above all, assuming the authority to correct the young. The young do not remain young long. If they find no correction during the brief and brilliant moment of their youth, they will have great trouble finding it thereafter, if, indeed, they ever manage to find it at all. With this in mind—this touchstone—and looking around this country, one trembles: or the young have been abandoned to the things that the Republic, their elders, have told them to buy. I am speaking, in the main, of the people who imagine themselves to be White—as the Republic imagines itself to be White—but a plague is no respecter of delusions.

Or, in other words, I am saying—and running the risk of being accused of chauvinism, especially by that merciless tribunal I carry around in my own head—that there was something in Black Atlanta's reaction to its prolonged ordeal that made me very proud. I know that sounds an easy thing to say—I did not go through it, after all. Yet, I stand by that statement, in spite of—or, even, perhaps, because of—the disputes, the accusations and counteraccusations, the genuine economic chasm and the presumed social divide, the very real weight and conundrum of the power of the State (and, for the State, a nigger is a nigger is a nigger, sometimes Mr. or Mrs. or Dr. Nigger), because those strident voices were, at bottom, controlled by the terror engulfing their children, and, therefore, themselves: the community. They were forced to recognize something that, on the basis of the evidence, is no longer real or vivid for the bulk of the Republic that imagines itself to be White: they could not live without their children any more than their children could live without them. They had not yet struck the bargain that nullified their birthright.

Yet, "our generation"—I am leaning on Andy again—was aware, mainly, "of the limits." Wayne was never aware of any limits—insofar, that is, as we can dare to speculate concerning the man, as distinguished from the accused. "Our" generation, therefore, like the generation before us, tried to give our children all that we had never had. And sometimes forgot, or sometimes lost sight of the fact—again, paraphrasing Andy— that the battle our forebears fought with "the limits" gave them the strength to raise us to be men and women. *This* strength is our real inheritance, and it must not be betrayed—certainly not for the Yankee-Western mess of pottage.

The Williams family went bankrupt in order to help their Icarus to fly. Only he never, it would seem, "learned to love himself." Something curdled in that energy; something hemorrhaged in what might have been genius. Something blocked his path to himself; therefore, inevitably, the path to others. It is unlikely, as well as irrelevant, that he is homosexual. He is, far more probably, not sexual at all: *he never learned to love himself.* This chill, as I read it, is the key to his mercurial performances on the witness stand, and intimidated the jury, as, indeed, it intimidates you and me. A person so authoritative and puny, so demanding and remote, is nothing less than terrifying—though he might not be, let me hasten to add, if you knew him as well or as little as you know your bachelor uncle, or your slightly kinky nephew. You have never had to study them on the witness stand.

There is, according to Andy, a disease peculiar to the Black community, called "sorriness." I am not a Southerner, and I had never heard this term before. It is a disease that attacks Black males. It is transmitted by Mama, whose instinct—and it is not hard to see why—is to protect the Black male from the devastation that threatens him the moment he declares himself a man. All of our mothers, and all of our women, live with this small, doom-laden bell in the skull, silent, waiting, or resounding, every hour of every day. Mama lays this burden on Sister, from whom she expects (or indicates she expects) far more than she expects from Brother; but one of the results of this all too comprehensible dynamic is that Brother may never grow up—in which case, the community has become an accomplice to the Republic.

Now, this dilemma has everything to do with the situation of the Black man in the American inferno, is positively the most crucial and anguished aspect of the Black American reality.

One is confronted, first of all, with the universal mystery of men—as we are, of a man, as he is; with the legend *and* the reality of the masculine force and the masculine role—though these last two realities are not always the same. Men would seem to dream more than women do—always have, it would seem, and, very probably, always will. They must, since they assume that their role is to alter and conquer reality. *If* women dream less than men—for men know very little about a woman's dreams—it is certainly because they are so swiftly confronted with the reality of men. They must accommodate this indispensable creature, who is, in so many ways, more fragile than a woman. Women know much more about men than men will ever know about women—which may, at bottom, be the only reason that the race has managed to survive so long.

In any case, the male cannot bear very much humiliation;

and he really *cannot* bear it, it obliterates him. All men know this about each other, which is one of the reasons that men can treat each other with such a vile, relentless, and endlessly inventive cruelty. Also, however, it must be added, with such depthless respect and love, conveyed, mainly, by grunts and blows. It has often seemed to me that men need each other in order to deal with women, and women, God knows, must need each other in order to deal with men.

Women manage, quite brilliantly, on the whole, and to stunning and unforeseeable effect, to survive and surmount being defined by others. They dismiss the definition, however dangerous or wounding it may be—or even, sometimes, find a way to utilize it—perhaps because they are not dreaming. But men are neither so supple nor so subtle. A man fights for his manhood: that's the bottom line. A man does not have, simply, the weapons of a woman. Mama must feed her children—that's another bottom line; and there is a level on which it can be said that she cannot afford to care how she does it.

But when a man cannot feed his women or his children, he finds it, literally, impossible to face them. The song says, *Now, when a woman gets the blues, Lord / She hangs her head and cries / But when a man gets the blues, Lord / He grabs a train and rides.*

For the action of the White Republic, in the lives of Black men, has been, and remains, emasculation. Hence, the Republic has absolutely no image, or standard, of masculinity to which any man, Black or White, can honorably aspire. What White men see when they look at Black men—insofar as they dare, or are able to perceive a Black as a man like themselves, like all men—I do not have the heart to conjecture. But, whatever this vision, or nightmare, is, it corrodes the life of the Republic on every level. A stranger to this planet might find the fact that there are any Black people at all still alive in America something to write home about. I, myself find it remarkable not that so many Black men were forced (and in so many ways!) to leave their families, but that so many remained and aided their issue to grow and flourish.

Yet, at bottom, and expressed in many different, halting ways, it was this question of *sorriness* as complicity that most disturbed the conscience of Atlanta's Black community. This so largely inexpressible disturbance had—has—been fermenting for a very long time now and it has lately been precipitated by the microbe of *integration*. For it is the false question of integration that, not at all paradoxically, has set the White and Black communities more than ever at a division and raised to so dangerous a pressure the real price, and meaning, of the history responsible for this division.

Let us backtrack, and, trying to be fair, remember that the Black demand was not for integration. Integration, as we could all testify, simply by looking at the colors of our skins, had, long ago, been accomplished. (As an old Black woman said to me, standing on her porch, in Alabama: "White people don't hate Black people—if they did, we'd all be Black.")

The Black demand was for desegregation, which is a legal, public, social matter: a demand that one be treated as a human being and not like a mule, or a dog. It was not even a direct demand for social justice: desegregation was a necessary first step in the Black journey toward that goal. It had absolutely nothing to do with the hope of becoming White. Desegregation demanded, simply, that Black people, and, especially, Black children, be recognized and treated as human beings by all of the institutions of the country in which they were born. Since, *I have done the State some service and they know it*, desegregation demanded that the State recognize, and act on, this irrefutable and irreducible truth.

As both Malcolm and Martin, in their not, after all, so very different ways, stated it—perceived it—this action was a necessity for the actual and spiritual health of the American State. And, furthermore, from the very beginning of this, the latest of the many struggles of Black people here, the questions of complicity and doom were raised. *I'm not sure I want to be integrated into a burning house.*

White Americans, however, bless their generous little hearts, are quite unable to imagine that there can be anyone, anywhere, who does not wish to be White, and are probably the most abject victims of history the world has ever seen, or will ever know. (Yes in spite of Iran, Ireland, England, Russia, and Jerusalem.) The Americans decided that desegregation meant integration, and, with this one word, smashed every Black institution in this country, with the single exception of the Black church.

And, in this, Black people were certainly accomplices, though I think the record shows, not only how little choice we had in the matter, but how deeply, and, even, dangerously, it sometimes divided us.

I was living in Washington, for example, in 1955, when downtown Washington had been desegregated for about a year. Almost none of the people I knew had yet tested these waters. I was with one of the first parties to go downtown—to "see" what would happen. I had not long returned from Paris, where it had taken time for me to learn to walk through a door without feeling that I was storming the Bastille. It was very strange, in my own country, to feel so menaced an interloper.

Eventually, one began to be accustomed to going "downtown." (This is partly because one's White business associates became accustomed to it.) For those who could—narrowly—afford it, going downtown was not so much a mark of status as a kind of vengeful, triumphant obligation. All of the energy of a powerful Republic had kept those doors locked in our faces for a very long time. Men had died, in order to break down those doors. And, if we could, now, walk through them and sit down at a table and be served, like any other citizen, it was not because the Republic had desired it but because *we* had willed it.

This was true enough, but the triumph was, also, a delusion, as many Black voices, at that hour, proclaimed. It cost the Republic nothing, after all, to soothe the ruffled feathers of the headwaiter (who might have been Black) or to find a new one: this "mingling" didn't (yet) cause stars to fall on Alabama. The reassuring conjunction of glass and cutlery contained not a hint of what was to happen, shortly, to our children, just down the road, in North Carolina, when, in less exclusive establishments, they were to ask for a cup of coffee. No. Nor was it as clear as it was, shortly, to become that the Republic, having fought for and sustained the separation of the races for so long, would transform the visible—as distinguished from the real—results of the Black insurrection into a propaganda medal for itself. Our presence, "downtown," resounded throughout the globe as proof that the leader of the "free" world was uncompromisingly devoted to freedom.

Integration was never considered a two-way street. Blacks went downtown, but Whites did not come uptown. This helped Black restaurants, in Atlanta, for example, to go bankrupt—we *just weren't there*—and such wealth as had been controlled by the Black citizens of Atlanta drastically and disastrously diminished. And bear in mind that we are discussing only the Southern city. Black wealth has no real resonance in the cities of the North.

The relationship of the Black "middle class" to the Black center of the city seemed to become, with integration, less and less organic. Though, were we discussing a Northern city, we would not be discussing this relationship at all: in New York, for example, this relationship had ended by the time of my adolescence. Two "race" riots, a war economy, and "progress" moved those Blacks who *could* move into the Bronx or Brooklyn or Jamaica, and, then, into suburbs much farther from the city than Atlanta's suburbs are from Atlanta. Or so it seemed, then: the Blacks were desperately trying to put a distance between themselves and misery. So it had seemed to a previous generation when they had been driven from the land into what they thought of as the cities of refuge and what the late E. Franklin Frazier anatomized as the "cities of destruction."

When I was in Atlanta in the fifties, though some Blacks rode buses (some trying and failing to be arrested for riding in the front) and some drove taxis and some drove cars—and many walked—we all seemed to be in hailing distance of each other, and in sight of a church or a poolroom or a bar. But now, neither Butler nor Auburn Street, for example, is what it was and, it seemed to me, the faces there, now, convey a pained and bewildered sense of having been abandoned. The well-to-do Blacks are far from the city's center, in the nearest suburbs. The Whites are in suburbs farther out, surrounding, encircling these: so that Black "middle class" is in a kind of limbo. They cannot move further out and they cannot move back in.

I had never before realized how simple a matter it is to create a suburb. Though I suddenly remembered how, during the voting crisis, Alabama had gerrymandered Tuskegee—since no one in Tuskegee had any difficulty with the literacy test—out of every known city except, perhaps, the New Jerusalem. "We have all," I remember a weary Black educator telling me, "suddenly been given a country place." In Atlanta, as in other cities, the land on which the Blacks had lived was reclaimed, for shopping malls and luxury hotels. In these installations, the grateful poor would—like their ancestors—clean basements, scrub toilet bowls, conquer kitchens, and carry trays. Nor are the Americans at all reluctant to describe this state of affairs as *progress*.

The optimistic ferocity of this cosmetic job is the principal, if not the only reason for the presence, in some cities, of the Black Mayor. It is absolutely safe to say that this phenomenon is, on the part of the Republic, cynical. It is a concession masking the face of power, which remains White. The presence of these beleaguered Black men—some of whom, after all, putting it brutally, may or may not be for sale—threatens the power of the Republic far less than would their absence.

Cities, in any event, are controlled by states, and these United States are controlled by the real aspirations of Washington. All governments, without exception, make only those concessions deemed absolutely necessary for the maintenance of the *status quo*; and if one really wishes to know how highly this Republic esteems Black freedom, one has only to watch the American performance in the world.

At the very beginning of what we will, now, call the Terror, it was, instinctively, assumed that this was but yet another convolution of the Ku Klux Klan—which would, oddly, perhaps, have been reassuring. But the fact, globally resounding, of a Black Administration rendered this assumption not only untenable, but craven. In the eyes of the world—to say nothing of the eyes of America—Americans had behaved with honor, and altered, upward, the status of the darker brother. America had, in fact, and with an unspeakable vengeance, done exactly the opposite, but the world had no way of knowing this and Americans had no reason to face it.

The situation of the Black American "minority" connects with the situation of the so-called "emerging" or "Third World" nations. These existed, until only yesterday, merely as a source of capital for the "developed" nations. The "vital" interests of the Western world were the riches extorted from the colonies: without this worldwide plunder, there could have been no Industrial Revolution. The colonies also had a therapeutic value for the colonizing societies in that these societies could, and did, dump their unruly youth and all their other misfits and rejects overseas, thus lessening the tensions or possibilities of rebellion on the mainland, and particularly in the newly industrialized and volatile metropoles. No colonizing power voluntarily surrendered this arrangement, and "independence" (like "integration") merely set in motion a complex legal and political machinery designed to camouflage and maintain the *status quo*.

None of the "emerging" nations has arrived at economic autonomy, and this is not because they are incapable of self-government, or are unable to count. One hears, for example, of the failure or the difficulty of their "export" market—which is not surprising, since this market is entirely controlled by the economic interests and arrangements of the West. On the "import" market, their situation is yet more precarious, since they can pay for these imports only in the Western currency that is being extracted from their flesh. A pound or a mark or a franc or a dollar or a diamond—or, even, a barrel of oil—does not, in an African village, have the meaning it acquires on the stock exchange. (Just as my ancestors did not have, in their village, the meaning their descendants were to acquire on the stock exchange.) No one can eat or otherwise use or consume a franc or a mark or a pound or a dollar or a diamond (or a barrel of oil) except, perhaps, as a bribe: these must be *invested*, be placed in the situation in which they multiply, in which they re-create each other, a situation in which *money makes money*. White South Africa, for example, is the most powerful nation on the dark continent (in good standing with the IMF), exporting, hourly, daily, tons of gold and diamonds and minerals, extorted out of the flesh of their Black slaves. And to whom is this plunder exported? To those who can pay for it, and it can be paid for only in the currency of the West. The source of this currency being, to put it kindly, cheap labor, those who produce it can never hope to benefit from it. It is locked in the vaults of other cities, and at the disposal of another people. Or, as William Buckley, who should certainly know, approvingly points out, "The dollars being paid . . . are of no use whatever to the foreign country . . . except to buy things from America, giving Americans jobs" (*International Herald-Tribune*, December 18–19, 1982).

If "honest toil and the magic of the marketplace"—to quote our quite magical and inestimable president Reagan—really created wealth, the Black people of this particular time and place and history would be among the wealthiest in the history of the human race. *Honest toil and the magic of the marketplace* sums up Black American history with a terrifying precision, and is the key to our continuing dilemma. Our first sight of

America was this marketplace and our legal existence, here, begins with the signature on the bill of sale.

Of course, it is true that many White people, including, certainly, the ancestors of many of our presidents, entered the country on similar terms—shipwrecks, criminals, and ladies fleeing to Salt Lake City to be married—but these all managed, and speedily enough, after all, to become White. They knew, at a glance, what would happen to them if they did *not* become White, and, by no means metaphorically, on which side such bread as they might hope to find would be buttered.

I say, to "become" White, for they had not been White before their arrival, any more than I, in Africa, had been Black. In Africa, I had been part of a tribe and a language and a nation. Just as the Native American—Columbus did *not* find a passage to India, but he knew how to sell a product—had been formed by, and was part of, a tribe and a language and a nation.

The concept of the nation, though, for those who had, now, been discovered had absolutely nothing to do with the recent and evolving European concept of the nation-state. *We* thought that the nation was sacred, as sacred as the land. *They* thought that the nation was plunder. *We* thought that we belonged to the nation. *They* thought that the nation belonged to them. Our ancestors were real to us, and so was our religion; but, to Europe, both appeared to have been sealed in great stone vaults. Thus, neither by their ancestors nor by their religion could they be corrected.

They certainly could not be corrected by Commerce, the only religion by which they lived—both Christian and Jew—as distinguished (and how!) from that which they professed. The European—a catchall term, referring, really, to the dooms of Capital, Christianity, and Color—became White, and the

African became Black—for commercial reasons. The price the White American paid for his ticket is not only in the so romanticized rupture between the so-called Old World and the so-called New, but in the terrified totality of his divorce from the most momentous creation of American life, his darker brother.

This divorce menaces, when it does not destroy, any possibility of the examined, or the moral life—since we are all brothers, and must learn from each other—and it weakens one's grasp of reality. It is impossible to look on a man and pretend that this man is a mule. It is impossible to couple with a Black woman and describe the child you have both created as a mulatto—either it's your child, or *a* child, or it isn't. It is impossible to pretend that you are not heir to, and, therefore, however inadequately or unwillingly, responsible to, and for, the time and place that give you life—without becoming, at very best, a dangerously disoriented human being. This ruthless dynamic affords some key to the disaster of the American private, social, and political life, to say nothing of America's "foreign" policy. Man cannot live by profit alone. But the situation of Black Americans has been created, and is dictated by this motive, and there is no other single detail of American life more revelatory of Americans and, absolutely, no level of American life it does not corrupt.

Blacks have never been, and are not now, really considered to be citizens here. Blacks exist, in the American imagination, and in relation to American institutions, in reference to the slave codes: the first legal recognition of our presence remains the most compelling. This is why each generation has been forced to insist, at mounting pressure—and higher cost—on "civil" rights: a revealing demand indeed, from a citizen! Only

the Native American (lo, the poor Indian) has been more bitterly blasphemed: "trying," as a White friend of mine once put
it, "to get *into* the hovels the Blacks are trying to get *out* of."

One speaks of the Blacks as *moving into* the cities, as
though this action were, somehow, both tardy and perverse.
But Blacks have been in the cities for a very long time, long
before, for example, the Irish immigrant arrived, looking for
one potato. And one likes to say that each immigrant, as he
arrived, encountered great obstacles and that each rose, in his
turn. This species of folklore—out of which Horatio Alger,
among others, was to make a killing—does not imply, but
very clearly states that America is the land of opportunity and
that Blacks, therefore, deserve their situation here. I no longer
really care why the authors of this self-serving fantasy cling to
it so ignobly. It is, nevertheless, worth pointing out that this
fable tells us, simply, that the economic and political base of the
city was determined entirely by immigrants who were in the
process of becoming White Americans. Whatever differences
the Irish, Greek, Pole, Italian, Finn, Norwegian, German—as
well as Jews, from all over the world—may have had between
themselves, they never, as entities, differed among themselves
concerning the role and the utility of the Black. They could
not afford to: those who dared were hounded out of the White
community (for it became *White* whenever *Black* was mentioned) as being *worse* than niggers—as being traitors, that
is, to the American Dream. (And that there were Blacks who
shared this dream, having—quite inevitably—deluded themselves into believing that they could be a part of it, is proven by
the fate of the West Indian Marcus Garvey, who was hounded
out of this country with the approval, if not the collusion, of
some of the then Negro leadership.) The White defector, or

dissident, perished between two communities, anathema to the White and distrusted by the Black.

That community that was in the process of becoming White could—and did—always bury its differences long enough to make certain that the Black could not rise to a place of sufficient recognition to threaten the structure of the labor union or the city or the state. And the saddest thing about this is that, even by the time I came along, searching for a watermelon in the streets of Harlem, there was nothing wicked about the White people who still lived in Harlem. But they could not see to what extent they themselves—having been manipulated into becoming White—were being manipulated by interests that cared no more about *their* lives than they cared about the lives of niggers. The Second World War forced the last of these European remnants over and out, and Harlem became an all-Black enclave. This reality was enforced by Mayor La Guardia (who had been born an Italian). La Guardia declared Harlem off-limits except, in effect, for those servicemen who had the right, or no choice but to live there—which was like declaring, in a paroxysm of honesty, that American democracy was an item for export only.

When White Americans, then, speak of the Blacks "moving into" the city, they are really referring to the city's first overt political recognition of the Black presence—or the first overt political recognition that was not (directly) accompanied by bloodshed. (It was preceded by the blinding, burning castration—the lynching—of Black Americans, returning home, in uniform.)

After the Second World War—and guided, perhaps, by La Guardia's courageous example during it—the city began

to create ghettos deliberately, instead of more or less haphaz-
ardly, and this was considered a victory for democracy.

Thus, for example, when Metropolitan Life built Stuyvesant
Town, on New York's 14th Street (*circa* 1948), it was considered, quite rightly, shameful that Black people, good enough
to die for America, were not good enough to live in Stuyvesant
Town. Metropolitan Life's commitment to democracy was not
so excessive as to cause them to open the portals of Stuyvesant
Town to Blacks. But, in the interests of democracy and social
peace, and with the certainty, after all, of turning a profit—they
had not been selling insurance all those years without discovering that there was always another dime to be extracted!—
Metropolitan Life built a housing project for Blacks, in Harlem,
called Riverton. This promptly became a part of the disaster
area in which it had been built, and various ones among the
merchants built more—I hate to think how many there are,
now (but the ghetto's problems are not addressed, still less
resolved, by causing anguish to reach into the sky). In any case,
the ghetto overflowed and Blacks began occupying more and
more of the city, encroaching section by embattled section: the
housing projects had failed to elicit the expected gratitude. The
Whites (*last best hope of earth*) fled from the Black or the non-
White face—pleading, heroically and revealingly enough, that
the Black presence would demolish property values.

This same White people said not a word while Robert
Moses and some friends of his turned New York into the dan-
gerous and decrepit parody of a metropolis that it is today.
They fled, from the niggers, to the suburbs.

Now they want to come back, and they will—as soon as
they have devised a way, once more, to get rid of the niggers.

Or—as they would, more gently, put it—to keep the nigger in his place.

It is terribly boring to have to say it—again—but it is the White flight and not the Black arrival that alters, or demolishes, property values. This arrival and departure is pure heaven for financiers and speculators: a ghetto is a source of great profit. No power under heaven can force the landlord to invest a penny in the upkeep of his property, and, if you think you can't get blood from a stone, watch salesmen of every description operating in the ghetto. Buy a *bedroom suite* in Harlem, or anything else, on the installment plan—I dare you: anything, including life insurance. Or just go shopping.

A Black neighborhood is a "high-risk" area *because* it is Black and *because* the bulk of the population is trapped there. And *when* they move—as, for example, when Blacks moved into the Bronx—they have created, simply, another "high-risk" area. A high-risk area is intolerably expensive because the money spent by the ghetto never returns to the ghetto. This means that those who batten on it—salesmen and landlords and lawyers, for example—must turn their profits with ruthless speed, for the territory occupied by the Blacks, or the non-White poor, swiftly becomes a kind of devastation.

This means that the citizens of the ghetto have absolutely no way of imposing their will on the city, still less on the State. No one is compelled to hear the needs of a captive population. Thus, the ghetto is condemned for the garbage in the streets, the condition of the buildings, which they do not own, the disaster of the schools—just as though the Black battles with the boards of education never happened, just as though schools exist independent of the neighborhoods in which they are found, and as though a Black person can walk into a bank and take out a loan or insure his property or his life on the same terms available to White people.

Furthermore, it is, perhaps, worth risking the observation—to make vivid the interlocking series of paradoxes that are the Black person's life in this country—that this particular aspect of the economic stranglehold is—or was—less true in Southern cities than in Northern cities. (The economic subjugation of the rural Black remains very nearly total.)

This is not because the American principle differed from the North to the South. It is because, in the cities, for a long time, the South had, or seemed to have, a *stable* population. That is, the South was certain that the nigger "knew" his place, the boundaries of which were, presumably, fixed forever by the existence of the Black "middle class." This "class" had an exceedingly complex usefulness in the Southern city, whereas it had virtually no resonance in the North: the Northern city demolished, simply, any meaningful relationship at all between the Black and the White communities—indeed, it is not too much to say that the Northern city demolished *all* communities. In the North, we lived in *neighbor(!)hoods.*

The usefulness, however, of the Black "middle class" to the Southern city—that is, to the maintenance of the White *status quo*—was, and had to be, so dubious a matter that it is fair to say that it existed, principally, in the imagination of the White South. (And, at that, it is important to repeat, *only* in the city: *I'm from Atlanta. I'm not from Georgia.*)

But this "class" was not created by the White imagination, but by the Black apprehension of their Black history and by those institutions that their ancestors had forged, the spirit, if not the form of which, they were to hand down to their children. They were models, all right, but not, as the

White South supposed, of the limits: they were witnesses to endless possibilities. So *their* elders had informed them, and *they* were the elders now. The performance of this "class," therefore, when confronted with the brutality to which their children were subjected—this, above all—turned the White Southern romance into an unreadable nightmare, and the results of this uneasiness are vindictively visible, in Atlanta, for example, or in Birmingham, which did not, a few years ago (before integration) have so many sections of town so visibly and vindictively resembling the wasteland of the Northern ghetto.

Finally, I think it is worth questioning the myth, in this country, concerning Black wealth. Wealth is not the same thing as affluence. Wealth, that is, is not the power to buy, but the power to dictate the terms of that so magical market-place—or, at the very least, to influence those terms. Wealth is the power to influence or to change the city's zoning laws or the insurance rates or the actuarial tables they apply to Blacks or the textbook industry or the father-to-son labor unions or the composition of the grand juries and the boards of education. Wealth is the power to make one's needs felt and to force a response to these needs. Though the American Jewish community, for example, can exert great influence over American policy toward Israel, Blacks have no overt influence at all on American policy toward South Africa.

To be fair, we can, of course, say that some doors appear to have opened for some Blacks. Without more carefully scrutinizing these doors (or what they open onto), we can say, certainly, that doors appear to be open for those who can afford the luxury items. This is why some American sociologists are beginning to insist that the problem is not "race" but "class"—

meaning those who find themselves on the bottom belong there.

The most visible of these are in the ghetto, and the city's only real interest in the ghetto is in its speediest possible deterioration.

Hence, the Black Mayor, interim caretaker of a valuable chunk of real estate, is in limbo. He has been placed, as we say in the streets, in a "trick bag," attempting to defend and represent a people who do not, for the state, exist. The state intends to reclaim the land, which is why the city has been abandoned, for this moment, to the Blacks.

Thus, for the moment, whatever happens in the city is the responsibility of those corralled there.

Bring out your dead:

Edward Hope Smith, 14. Reported missing July 20, 1979. Found dead on July 28 of gunshot wounds along a road in a wooded area.

Bring out your dead:

Alfred James Evans, 13. Last seen July 25, 1979, waiting to catch a bus. Police identified Evans's body October 13, 1980, after it was found July 28 near the body of Edward Hope Smith. Strangulation.

Bring out your dead:

Milton Harvey, 14. Last seen September 1979. Found dead November 1979. Cause of death: undetermined.

Bring out your dead:

Yusef Ali Bell, 9. Last seen October 1979. Strangled.

Angel Lanier, 12. Last seen March 1980. Found March 1980. Strangled.

Jeffrey L. Mathis, 10. Last seen March 1980. Found February 1981. Cause of death: undetermined.

Eric Middlebrooks, 14. Last seen May 1980. Found May 1980. Cause of death: head injury.

Christopher P. Richardson, 11. Last seen June 1980. Cause of death: undetermined.

Latonya Wilson, 7. Last seen June 1980. Found October 1980. Cause of death: undetermined.

Aaron D. Wyche, 10. Last seen June 1980. Found June 1980. Asphyxiation.

Anthony Bernard Carter, 9. Last seen July 1980. Found July 1980. Stabbed.

Earl Lee Terrell, 10. Last seen July 1980. Found January 1981. Cause of death: undetermined.

Clifford Jones, 13. Last seen August 1980. Found 1980. Strangled . . .

Before we begin to speculate as to what, in the foregoing, can be said to constitute a "pattern," it is important to point out that it was the thirteenth murder—that of Clifford Jones—that precipitated the (official) hue and cry. Jones, like Emmett Till, in 1955—a comparison I wish neither to force nor avoid—was an out-of-state visitor from what we still, quaintly, call the North. Had he been a "Mississippi boy," his bones might yet be irrecoverable at the bottom of the river, or nourishing the earth of various and celebrated Mississippi plantations, to speak only of Mississippi, and saying nothing of subsidies, and without insisting on the official and lethal power of the South- ern states in the august and marble halls of Washington.

The *only* reason, after all, that we have heard of Emmett Till is that he happened to come whistling down the road—an obscure country road—at the very moment the road found itself most threatened: at the very beginning of the segregation- desegregation—not yet integration—crisis, under the knell of the Supreme Court's *all deliberate speed*, when various "moder- ate" Southern governors were asking Black people to segregate themselves, *for the good of both races*, and when the President of the United States was, on this subject, so eloquently silent that one *knew* that, in his heart, he did not approve of a mon- grelization of the races.

In this harsh light and harsher silence, the murder of the boy became a spiritual and patriotic duty. It is impossible to know what might have happened had Authority felt, or dared suggest, that the darker brother has every right to be here, and nothing whatever to prove. No American president has ever unequivocally stated this—certainly not, for example, Lincoln, who was simply determined to preserve the Union, with slavery or without it; nor Kennedy, who addressed Mississippi on the night that James Meredith was carried into Ole Miss as though there are no Black people in Mississippi; nor Roosevelt, who could not "take [the] chance" of fighting for an anti-lynch law. As concerns all the other presidents, with the possible (but meaningless) exception of Thomas Jefferson, Blacks have never had any human reality at all. (Carter is another exception—a real exception, and so was Johnson, in an entirely different way; but both are, exquisitely, the exceptions that prove the rule.)

The moral vacuum of any society immediately creates an actual social chaos. This vacuum is that space of confusion in which the word is not suited to the action, nor intended to be— in which the action is not suited to the word, nor intended to be. It is that space in which everyone, helplessly, has something to hide, in which every man's hand—helplessly—is against his brother: that space in which we dare not recognize that our birthright is to love each other.

The real meaning and history of Manifest Destiny, for example, is nothing less than calculated and deliberate genocide. But American folklore, which has seduced American history into a radiant stupor, transforms this slaughter into a heroic legend. Since the legend has obliterated the truth, and since the legend controls what is left of the American imagination, it is all but impossible for the White North American really to understand why, for example, in Salt Lake City, such *Indians* as may intrude on his/her attention are to be found in front of the state liquor store. Nor does he question the validity of or reason for a *state* liquor store, nor why he/she, free, white, and over twenty-one, can drink, legally, only at home or in one of the many many many "private" clubs that flourish in the

Mormon capital. His presumed dominance blinds him to the rigors of his own captivity. He cannot possibly see himself as others—the subjugated—see him. He understands an "Indian" uprising as little as he understands "crime in the streets": *crime in the streets* being the action, entirely, of the irresponsibly discontented and ungrateful *Negro*.

The moral vacuum results in the betrayal of the social contract, and, when this contract is broken, Chaos is at everyone's door.

This chaos, like a plague, is no respecter of persons, tribes, or aspirations—so one must recognize (again) that it is not, in itself, enough to be Black. Or, in other words, it is no longer necessary—and, very shortly, will no longer be possible—for Blacks to define themselves merely in opposition to the European vocabulary. This vocabulary, precisely to the extent that it cannot encompass the Black experience, fails to confront, still less translate the White experience, and the Black experience lives outside this language, and in spite of it.

If I write you a letter, for example, I am trying to tell you something or ask you something—whatever the message, it can be, finally, only myself, hoping to be delivered. If I speak to you, I want you to hear me—to hear *me*—and to see me. Speech and language, however ceremonious, complex, and convoluted, are a way of revealing one's nakedness; and this revelation is, really, our only human hope. But this hope is strangled if one, or both of us, is lying.

Most White North Americans are always lying to, and concerning, their darker brother, which means that they are always lying to themselves. Who doubts me has only to consider the state of the Union.

White North Americans live in a country that, in the

generality, and, emphatically, in action, believes that nothing is more important than being White. Black North Americans, trapped on the same territory, and under what can, perhaps, best be described as different conditions of servitude, also concluded that it was important to be White—nothing could have been more obvious. The question was how to go about it.

So, one watched the people made *White* by a voyage. the Savage called them the people from heaven. And they *were* many colors but they were not White.

What were they, then? What they were was, at once, a menacing, overwhelming, inescapable Presence and an echoing, intolerable Absence. This was the model—the Word made flesh—that one had no choice but to emulate, please, outwit, pity, despise, hate, and sometimes kill and sometimes love, as long as the sun rose and set. Every hour was lived in the shadow of death, not only, or merely, one's own. Mother, daughter, nieces, the womenfolk, uncle, nephew, brother, the father and the son. And these relations, realities, having no social recognition or legal validity, had, daily, to be caressed, like contraband, or staked out as hopefully as a claim.

It is a very grave matter to be forced to imitate a people for whom you know—which is the price of your performance and survival—you do not exist. It is hard to imitate a people whose existence appears, mainly, to be made tolerable by their bottomless gratitude that they are not, thank heaven, *you.* One is confronted with a chasm. And this void is not to be compared—for example—with the Irish situation in the hands of the English, for they both, at least as the Irish supposed, looked like the children of the same God. Who could possibly have warned the Irish of the price they were to pay for an

English monarch's bill of divorcement? Nor is the Black situation in the West, and, more particularly, in North America, to be compared with that of the Jew, in Germany. The German Jew had no reason to suppose that he was not German any more than he had any reason to suppose that Germany was not Civilized: *all* White people are, by definition, Civilized. He had fought and died for the Fatherland, his blood was in that soil, as well as his honor, and his children's hope. He could not possibly have imagined that a social contract of sacred dimensions could be so viciously broken. *Mene, mene, tekel, upharsin* had not yet translated itself into so unspeakable a confrontation between the Chosen People and the Master Race.

The social contract smashed in Germany will rank forever, quite beyond time's power to obliterate or the human or divine power to forgive, among the most abominable moments in the history of the human being. It also exposed, forever, and exploded, the moral authenticity of the Judeo-Christian ethic and marks the end of the moral authority of the Western world. (Yes: mark my words.) The Western world understood the German Chancellor's need for *Lebensraum* very well and did nothing to thwart it until *his* living space interfered with *their* living space. The decimation of the dissidents, the burning of the books, the incarceration and subsequent prolonged slaughter of the gypsies, such Blacks as the Third Reich could find, the homosexuals, and the Jews, elicited nothing more from the Civilized world than a flood of crocodile tears and a reexamination of trade agreements. The West went to war against the monster the West had created, in self-defense and *for no other reason*.

The auction block is the platform on which I entered the

Civilized world. Nothing that has happened since, from South Africa to El Salvador, indicates that the Western world has any real quarrel with slavery.

Since we, the Blacks, did not look White, we could hope to arrive at this state only by imitation. (The idea of becoming White by fornication came, by precept and example, later. The fact that Black men and women surmounted this most incredible passage of the diaspora is the subject of another essay, or, as I believe, another pen.)

One can imitate one thing only—reality. One can mime the wind, or the effects of the wind, or fire, but one must know that wind and fire are merciless. To imitate another human being is to translate, interpret, the confession contained in every gesture, every trick and tone of voice—that is what every human being is about; that is what love is about. In the case of the Black attempting to imitate the White, it became clear, at once, that they were confronted, merely, with a surface. They could imitate only this surface, but this surface was not the person. There was no reason, and, indeed, no way, to imitate the depths. They recognized the depths at once, in the same way that one perceives the difference between one child and another. Furthermore, the Black man/woman lived with, and in those depths, all day, all seasons, all the lifetime long: a vast amount of the precision of the Black North American's style comes out of his apprehension that he was imitating an imitation.

He had almost certainly never seen, for example, the aristocrat whom Scarlett's daddy, far from home, had taken as a model, but he knew that Scarlett's daddy was no aristocrat. (He, the Black, was no stranger to aristocrats; perhaps he had been sold by one.) Scarlett's daddy was just a displaced—perhaps mostly drunken, perhaps mostly sober—peasant who could hardly, any longer, do a day's work if his life had depended on it, and Scarlett was just an unloved—or loved—unlovable, or lovable, hysterical, or winning child. Her brother tended to piss in bed, might or might not grow up to be a man (but the odds were not in his favor); her cousin was always sniffing around the slave quarters in which the mistress saw, daily, her husband's children. And everyone pretended that Black people were blind and could not see the reality all around them—in spite of the fact that this reality held over Black people, daily, the power of life or death.

There was no way to imitate this crushing physical presence that was ruled by a total moral vacuum, just as Blacks did not become Christians by imitating slaveholders. What evolved was what appeared to be a strategy for safety. White people read this seeming subservience as indicating the Black need for *acceptance* but Black people described it as *bowing mighty low.*

Or, in other words, the truth concerning the White North American experience is to be deciphered in the hieroglyphic lashed onto the Black man's back—there, and in the continuing fate of the last of the Mohicans: and this truth cannot be overcome until it is confronted.

Therefore, when I say that it will, presently, not be enough to be Black, I am not only attempting to suggest our imminent and global responsibilities as the most notorious and important of all African contributions to the West, I am also stating that our actual and moral alternatives have never been, and are not now, simply at the mercy of the North American inferno.

The adolescent, Till, was murdered by two White North American males—the issue of European emigrants, born south of the Canadian border—for *whistling* at a White woman.

Now, in some other place and time—in that universal beginning and wonder of all lives—they might have been able to recognize themselves in the boy, have laughed with him, and at him, and been able to correct him by remembering how they themselves had whistled—in that time, now so irrecoverably behind White North Americans, when a woman was not merely White, but a woman, and no boy was merely Black, but a *boy*, when all boys were the responsibility of all men.

For the boy was crowing like a cock and signaling that he was proud and happy to be, and have one—which is the very definition of innocence and terror, as all men should know. But the boy was Black and so they had to kill him—of course. They were judged by a jury of their peers to be innocent. Nor did they lose their jobs: I think that one of the brothers was promoted.

The good Lord alone knows what happened to the womanhood of the so vindictively prized woman.

Yusef Ali Bell, age nine, was the fourth victim and it was his mother, Ms. Camille Bell, who began the Stop the Murders Mothers' Committee. It was she, apparently, who first perceived not so much a "pattern" as a mortal threat and she who raised the hue and cry.

Authority, and/or bureaucracy, responded at its usual snaillike pace: the missing children were, for a while, lumped together as runaways, or "hustlers." This description, or, more precisely, this reaction, reveals enormities concerning what is generally expected of the children, to say nothing of the parents, who fall beneath the economic level that, in principle, makes possible a measure of social autonomy. It must also be added, to be fair, that a *missing* or *runaway* child does not, immediately, translate itself, in the mind, as a murdered child (not even when the child's body has been found). No degree of imagination or disciplined power of rehearsal can prepare anyone for the unspeakable; and there can be nothing more unspeakable—nor, alas, very probably, more common—than the violence inflicted on children.

It is absolutely impossible for Authority or bureaucracy to scent danger as swiftly as does the menaced human being. Authority can scent danger only to itself. It demands a crisis of whatever proportions before the private danger can be perceived as menacing the public safety. For you, or for me, for example, the missing child distorts, totally, the universe, but, for Authority, it is a statistic and, for bureaucracy, a detail. Only when these details and statistics begin to multiply is a public danger perceived.

Furthermore, in the present case, the Black people of Atlanta found themselves, today, and under the intolerably brutal and indifferent public light, living nothing less than the ancestral, daily, historical truth of Black life in this country. (*Ancestral* and *daily* are synonyms and *historical* does not refer to that spotless mirror in which the bulk of White North Americans imagine they see their faces.)

It is an error to underestimate the private and collective memory of the most brutal—and, until today, prolonged—of human dispersals, or diasporas. It was only the day before yesterday, after all, that Black children belonged not to their parents, but to the fluctuations of the stock exchange: indeed, if one looks around this country, or this world, today, that last statement may strike one as being indefensibly optimistic.

On the assumption, then, that Authority, in Atlanta, is Black, it could be assumed by that private and collective memory, precisely, which registers that it was not only bought or kidnapped, but *sold*; that Black people were indifferent to the fate of the children, and responded, when they did, less out of a concern for the children than a concern for the continued commercial viability of the city too busy to hate.

There is nothing new about such priorities, nor do these priorities have a color line. I think it is important to face this truth and it will become, steadily, globally, more important as this century nears its end. On the other hand, in the present case—Atlanta—I must tell you that I do not share this accusatory assumption. I do not share it because it reveals the dimensions of that trap in which the White North American, quite helplessly, and, indeed, quite, as it were, without malice, intends to keep the Black. He has no choice. To face the Black man is to be forced to face himself.

There is a striking difference of emphasis between the heirs of Europe and the heirs of Africa. I say *emphasis* because the human inheritance is simply that, human, and universal, imposing on all human beings the necessity of treating each other as sacred. Though *both read the Bible, day and night*, and both believe in conquest, one believes in safety. The proof is in our songs and in the lives we lead and the price we pay.

The crisis in Atlanta cannot, for example, really be compared to the situation we encounter in Thomas Mann's *Death in Venice. Death in Venice* is not merely the study of an aging, ego-ridden, European artist, surrendering, in Venice, to the inscrutable passions of his unlived life. This life would appear to be inscrutable and unlived because of an appalling lack of witnesses: the artist is admired, and to a crushing extent, but no one has ever corrected the man. His unlived life takes its revenge and surfaces in the form of an adolescent boy, who exists, almost entirely, in the man's imagination. Compelled by his journey toward his receding mirage, he lingers in Venice, and dies. The story is centered on a self not so much diminished or irrecoverable or unknown as *static*: he will never sing, *The very day I thought I was lost, my dungeon shook—and my chains fell off!* And the horror of his unlived life and unloved love is conveyed by the fact that there is a plague raging in Venice, and every hour he spends there brings him closer to death. He does not, as you or I might do, pack his bags and pick up his bed, or his boy, and walk: no, he expires, elaborately, on the beach, supine victim, finally, of the icy workings of the chamber of commerce.

For, no one in Venice is about to announce a plague at the very height of the season. To recognize and declare a plague will bring about the ruin of the city, ruin by no means metaphorical. Taxi drivers will not drive, maids will have no function, cooks will not collect leftovers for their families, waiters will not wait and wine will not be poured. It does not, in Mann's fable, appear to be important that all of these people may be stricken and die. They appear to believe that they will, somehow, outlive it, and they are, probably, after all, right: they have before. A plague may be no respecter of persons, but that means, only, that there are two sides to every coin.

The difference of emphasis that I am trying to situate would seem to me to result in—or is, perhaps, produced by—a chilling view of human isolation. I am not attempting to deny the truth or the enormity of this isolation: each of us is unique, irreplaceable, and passing through. But, it seems to me that it is precisely our irreplaceability, uniqueness, mortality, that is the splendor of the human connection. That isolation and death are certain and universal clarifies our responsibility.

Love, life, and death are not, as some would put it, "head

games." I remember, for example, a point in my life when I was asked to consider involving myself in the production of a play based on *Oedipus Rex*. The modern, or updated, script occurred in a Polish concentration camp during the reign of the Third Reich. *Oedipus Rex* is the play that the camp's theatrical troupe will perform for Christmas.

The principal role, Oedipus, is to be played by an actor who is the son of a man and a woman who are prisoners in this same camp. But none of these three know this: each one of them assumes that the other two are dead. The Commandant, who knows their identities, has decided that it will be amusing to have these three actually live, unwittingly, the Oedipus drama. The son is set up to attempt to escape by killing the one guard on duty on a certain night. This guard is, of course, his father, who has been instructed to keep his back to the prisoner and allow him to escape. The prisoner knows only that he must shoot him. The mother is informed that her son is alive and, though no longer as well as he was, is living in this place. She is also informed that her son will be brought into her pitch-black cell and that she, disguised, will pretend to be the whore he has been promised. If she thwarts the copulation by any deed or sign, not she, but her son will be put to death. And, then, the son is confronted with what he has done as the play is about to be performed.

I did not believe a word of this play. I was repelled by the intellectual arrogance of the conceit—an arrogance that revealed, it seemed to me, an appalling contempt for the human being. (The arrogance of the author seemed very like that of the Commandant.) I did not disbelieve the horror—we live in an age the horror of which can scarcely, if at all, be described—but I did not believe this report. I did not believe that human beings could be, unwittingly, so manipulated. I did not believe that my father or my mother or their son could become as witlessly ruthless as a goat. Though I had seen horrors, and horrors enough, madness, suicide, heard the junkie's howl, and encountered many forms of murder, I had never encountered anyone who did not, somewhere, deep within the inaccessible cave, *know* something of the dreadful algebra of the journey—the "trip"—that had brought him/her to the place from which there was no deliverance.

And if one wishes to say—true enough, fair enough—that I was unable to see this because I was unwilling to imagine it, this merely brings us back to my starting point, which, I have suggested, ineptly enough, perhaps, is the striking difference of emphasis—and I am deliberately avoiding the word, *perception*—between the heirs of Europe and the heirs of Africa: the different vantage points from which our lives are apprehended. For a life is controlled and a civilization defined by what each takes life to be. And what we take life to be is what our lives become.

Venice, in any case, lacked, on the one hand, Atlanta's beleaguered Black Administration, and, on the other hand, perhaps even more crucially, it lacked Ms. Camille Bell.

I met Ms. Bell twice or three times, briefly and publicly, and I found her to be an impressive and very moving woman. She was blunt and handsome, clearheaded, outgoing. I *could* not interview her because I simply did not know what to say to the mother of a murdered child, still less what to ask. I was certain that some kind of ghoulish curiosity was in my eyes and in my voice. I, mainly, listened. Her concern was what she took to be the official indifference to the slaughter of the children, which connected, for her, with the economic status of the victims. I had no choice but to suspend judgment. (I have never, in all my journeys, felt more of an interloper, a stranger, than I felt in Atlanta, in connection with this case, and I sometimes cursed the editor whose brainstorm this had been.)

However, she knew far more about this case and this city than I—crucially, far more about the city. And I have described her as outgoing, which is certainly the impression she made on me. But I also felt that she was holding herself together with a safety pin, was forcing herself to be clear, articulate, active—to keep moving, one step ahead of the sledgehammer of grief. This is really why I couldn't ask her anything, but this quicksilver tension invested her testimony, or, more accurately, her point of view, with great authority. She was direct and could be extremely caustic, but she wasn't self-pitying and she wasn't mean and her grief was not hers alone. Her grief connected her with the other mothers and families, connected her, it seemed to me, with responsibility.

But, due, no doubt, to her caustic tongue—she referred to the Mayor as "the fat boy"—she was far from being the most popular lady in Atlanta. No one said anything directly against her, partly, I finally decided, because no one knew very much about her. One was allowed to assume, nevertheless, that she was misguided and irresponsible and not above turning her son's murder into a public and financial triumph for herself. I must say that I found this silent suggestion, to say the very least, unlikely. She didn't impress me as having that particular kind of stamina or being capable of harboring such a motive. She impressed me as meaning exactly what she said.

And this general reaction to Ms. Bell caused me to look not at her, but around me. I was astounded, for example, that so many people appeared to believe that Wayne Williams was guilty—were *relieved* to think of him as guilty. It was, precisely, this *relief* that caused in me a steady chilled wonder, less concerning the accused than those who were so anxious to accuse and condemn him. The accused may be guilty, for all I know, but I fail to see his guilt as proven. Others may see American progress in economic, racial, and social affairs—I do not. I pray to be proven wrong, but I see the opposite, with murderous implications, and not only in North America.

The economic dividing lines among the people trapped in the Atlanta nightmare may, finally, on a coming day, interpret it. For reasons involving guilt, terror, and bewilderment, the economic disparity between the runaway children and those relatively more secure—economically—began to be leaned on as a means both of avoiding and confronting the nightmare. Indeed, I think it is probable that never before had this question so brutally menaced Atlanta's Black community.

Up until, and during, that betrayed and co-opted insurrection that American folklore has trivialized into "the civil rights movement," the porter and the banker and the dentist all knew that they needed each other. Economic and societal rigors being what they are, it cannot be said that they were intimate, but each knew where to find the other. The social details, the habits, of integration, created not a divorce, but a distance. One will not give a friendly nod to the porter while dining out at the Peachtree Plaza, because the porter won't be there. Of course, the poverty of the porter eventually precipitates the bankruptcy of the banker and the dentist, but what I am saying, now, is that the myth of integration attacked and began to unravel a tightly woven social fabric. And there could be no more devastating proof of this assault than the slaughter of the children.

This is certainly among the principal reasons that Camille Bell seemed, for so many, an embarrassment. I had the feeling that this was less because of her intransigent position than the fact that she had presumed to take any position at all.

Her position, however one judged it, was consistent. "The parents of the children who are murdered and who are missing contend that no one has the right, the authorization, or the authority to collect funds for the parents except the committee that the parents themselves have set up."

This is a very clear statement, which is unforgivable enough. It is, also, since none of the mothers rose up to repudiate it, subversive—as subversive, say, as the action, example, and premise of *Antigone*. It was being addressed to some formidable people and coalitions, some White and some Black, but this statement also addressed and defied the sovereign state of Georgia and the Republic for which it stands.

STATE IS ASKED TO PROSECUTE FUND SOLICITORS IN ATLANTA is the headline of a June 1, 1981, *New York Times* article. And the Governor's Office of Consumer Affairs had indeed warned the Committee to Stop Children's Murders that they were liable to prosecution on both civil and criminal charges.

The state of Georgia had never before exhibited so intense an interest in Black life or Black death. And this threat, coming from the Governor of the state, was not really aimed at the parents of the murdered children but at the Administration of the city of Atlanta. I find it fascinating, furthermore, that it should issue from the Office of Consumer Affairs—an office not created, presumably, to involve itself with murder, or the aftermath of murder. The Office of Consumer Affairs is, in principle, as removed from such bloody matters as the

Department of Agriculture. In principle, however, by all accounts, a vast amount of money poured into the state and the city during his time, creating havoc and embarrassment. Not only, for example, for the people who did not quite know how to look or dress or behave, at the Sammy Davis, Jr., benefit. Who in the world can blame them, finding themselves under the very real obligation of *buck-dancing on the graves*? Your presence is required—that is really all that you know. A holocaust is no respecter of mirrors. You act as you can, or as you must. But you must be present.

This was not, however, the concern of the state. The state held that the Committee to Stop Children's Murders violated Georgia law as concerned charitable solicitations. This may strike one as a somewhat callous position to take, concerning such a devastation—*charitable*, indeed!—but it makes perfect (if somewhat chilling) sense. For what Camille Bell's committee had done was to alert the nation and the world to the fact that there was indeed a plague raging in the city too busy to hate.

Years ago, after the slaughter of the four little girls in the Birmingham Sunday school, Ruby Dee, Ossie Davis, John O. Killens, Odetta, the late Louis Lomax, and some others, including me, rented New York's Town Hall to demand that Christmas, that year, be declared a day of mourning. We held that a Christian nation had no right to celebrate the birthday of the Prince of Peace before it made an attempt to atone.

The parents of the children were onstage with us. They were not there on holiday, though we hoped, certainly, that they would see some of the sights of New York—would have, as we clumsily put it, a "good time." Perhaps they did manage to see Radio City or Madison Square Garden: the prospect did not appear to thrill them. They were not there on holiday. They were there as witnesses. We hoped that we could do whatever was humanly possible in the brutally brief time that we had—but they were engulfed by a silence that no one could enter.

And, of course, doing all this cost money. No doubt, some of the parents bought something. I hope so.

The committee brought the Atlanta Administration under attack—for there appears to have been no real reaction to the murders before the committee was formed—not so much from those on the bottom, whose cry is rarely heard, but from the top. From the state of Georgia, in fact, which, ultimately, controls the city of Atlanta. More than that: Georgia is controlled by Washington, even, or perhaps especially, when it can seem to be the other way around.

Thus, the impenetrable meeting at the Governor's mansion—or, at any rate, with the Governor—comes about. When I first arrived in Atlanta, I knew nothing of this meeting. Then, I encountered so many people who *had not been there* that I realized that this meeting must have taken place.

Slaton is not among the people who were not there—for the reason that D.A. Slaton, who was exceedingly cordial, made it very clear that he was not going to discuss the case with me at all.

Nevertheless, as in an ancient Boris Karloff movie, such a meeting apparently took place. Bereft as I am of witnesses, I can only conjecture, after the fact. But it was after the meeting with the Governor, or simultaneously, that President Reagan, Vice President Bush, and the FBI entered the case. "We never asked for any money, except from Reagan," one official tells me, and: "*We* asked for the FBI."

"Which," a friend of mine tells me, "seems a little odd, if you remember the FBI and us, during the civil rights days."

Well. Yes and no. It depends on how one reads the motive. I do not read the motive as having anything to do with any concern for the dead children—or, for that matter, the living. I read the motive as being dictated by the necessity of stifling an incipient scandal in order to protect the magic of the market-place. There was, I am told, "zero fall-off" in business: conventioneers continued to arrive, in their cheerful thousands, filling up the hotels, the bars, and the shopping malls. Somewhat less conveniently, money came pouring into the Mayor's office from fifty states and seven continents—sometimes nickels and dimes and pennies from schoolchildren—and the Mayor's office acknowledged every contribution and kept an accounting of every penny. They were forced to use a triple accounting system and the money went to, or was the cornerstone of, the Atlanta Children's Foundation.

In spite of all this, then, *Atlanta has prospered, has grown. We're an American city. Our motto is resurgence.*

And the children were "so closely watched." For example, a Black man, driving, happened to stop beside a car containing a White couple and a Black child. He gave chase, shouting, and, in one way or another, the car was forced to stop. But the boy and the couple had perfectly valid reasons for being together: "everything," I was told, "turned out to be normal."

"The issue," says another, "overtook our lives."

This, I think, cannot be doubted. I am a partial witness to the truth of that statement. When the Balthazar child disappeared, one of the last people to see him was his barber. The child was running an errand and waved as he passed by the barbershop window and was never seen again, alive. And the barber told me how much he had loved and admired young Patrick Balthazar, who had come from New Orleans to live with his father.

Yet, I talked to the father, too, who was utterly devastated by what he took to be the official indifference to the life and death of his son. Grief, as we know, translates very easily into rage—rage, in fact, at heaven. But, just the same, his face and his voice made me remember someone else telling me that Atlanta has "White neighborhoods, Black neighborhoods—but not *these* neighborhoods!"

For the children came, mainly, from Atlanta's lowest economic stratum. This means that they were strangers to safety, for, in the brutal generality, only the poor watch over the poor. The poor do not exist for others, except as an inconvenience or a threat or an economic or sometimes missionary or sometimes genuinely moral opportunity. *The poor ye have with you always*; indeed, but never, in the main, to be seen, and never, certainly, as we should know by now, to be heard.

The poor do not awaken to breakfast. They wake up to whatever there is. They do not, necessarily, step into a shower or take a bath: the plumbing of the poor is as unpredictable as the political fortunes of an "emerging" nation. They may or may not dress and go to work: they may, eventually, find it intolerably corrosive to look for work. Lunch may or may not happen. Your armpits and your socks and your feet may stink. You are never absolutely certain that they don't, no matter how cleverly you manipulate the faucet, with what industry you lay your underwear out to dry; and emptying one's bladder or one's bowels can present monumental problems. This is true for the father, which is the principal reason he is so often absent, and it is true for the son. If I say that the poor are strangers to safety, it is not only because others look on the poor with such a defensive disdain, it is also because the poor cannot bear the condescension and pity they see in the eyes of others. Or imagine that they see—it comes to the same thing. You smell your odor, as it were, in the other's eyes. And this is intolerably compounded if you are poor, young, and Black.

No amount of surveillance could have saved the children from the Omni, for example—since it was there. The name (I have reported elsewhere) is scarcely more ambitious than the place, which is a kind of frozen, enclosed suburb. It is about five minutes away from a sprawling, poor Black neighborhood, called Vine City. A child can walk here from his home in less than five minutes; some of the murdered children were last seen in this place.

One enters through a galaxy of shopwindows selling clothes that your momma and your papa can't buy; the entire place is honeycombed with overpriced tourist items—I was about to say overpriced tourists. There are several levels. One finds oneself standing beneath an enormous dome and the building stretches above one, tier by tier. Among the establishments on the ground level, there is a "French" bakery and a pinball, video-game arcade—a space that contains a staggering array and variety of game machines. In the center of all this is a tremendous open ice-skating rink (*since closed*) and at the opposite end of the floor, facing the arcade, is the movie house, a complex containing, I believe, six theatres. This vast space is nothing less than a magnet for children and for those who prey on children. And, in spite of the curfew, here were the boys—looking for a narcotic, for money for the movies, for the pinball machines, for the skating rink: looking for change.

Looking for *a* change.

For the only "pattern" I could discern in the murders was that the victims were young Black males—there were also two Black female children—living in the purgatory, or the eternity, of poverty. To be poor and Black in a country so rich and White is to judge oneself very harshly and it means that one has nothing to lose. Why not get into the friendly car? What's the worst that can happen? For a poor child is, also, a very lonely child.

There were, I am told, no other cases that "fit the pattern" once Wayne Williams was arrested. There were no murders that "fit the pattern" while he was on trial. But, as I was not told that murder in Atlanta had ceased with the arrest and trial of Wayne Williams, I began to be more and more disturbed by this—for me—increasingly elusive "pattern." The police had been looking for a "Vietnam veteran type," but, once the FBI entered the case, they kept getting "leads," according to Slaton, that pointed to Wayne Williams.

But what was one to make of a "pattern" that included, as cause of death, gunshot wounds, strangulation, head injury, stabbed, asphyxiation, and undetermined? Particularly if this was assumed to be the work of one man.

One boy's death, for example, was attributed to asphyxiation: his body had been found in the weeds beneath the railroad tracks. It had been suggested that the boy had fallen off this viaduct while walking on the ledge. I walked this viaduct. It did not seem to me that a fall from this height would necessarily be mortal. The railing, or the ledge, was of heavy thick metal, wide enough for a playful kid to walk on. This barrier came just below my shoulders. The boy had been smaller than I, and would have had to make a very determined effort to climb up on that ledge. His family said, however, that the boy was terrified of heights and would never have dreamed of amusing himself that way. Someone, then, would have had to lift him and throw him over. Assuming that he was still alive when he landed in the weeds, one can agree, certainly, that he was asphyxiated; yet it seemed to me a somewhat inadequate way of describing the cause of death.

On the other hand, official language really has no choice but to be that and is not meant to reveal so much as to distract and, as it were, console. It is also under the necessity of attempting to preserve the social contract and the public peace. But, in the present case, this limitation meant that the official reassurance that there were no murders that "fit the pattern" once Williams was arrested was met with a profoundly uneasy and not always silent skepticism.

When I first came to Atlanta, the people under the greatest suspicion were policemen and preachers. This is not hard to understand (so I tried to reassure myself) given their authority and (visible) freedom of movement in the community. Yet, there was something eerie about this reaction, and infectious, like catching a friend's cold. Having grown up with preachers, and having been one myself, I can claim, I think, to know something of the hazards (and the beauty) of the ministry. In my youth, and during my time in the pulpit, though we knew that Reverend So-and-So was not exactly what he claimed to be—for example, he played the numbers, was a little too fond of the wine and the laying on of hands—we never really doubted the reality of his ministry. He was never suspected of doing any deliberate harm to the community—even though, for the most part, it seemed beyond his power to do us any particular good. For the most part, there were some who did a great deal of good for us, including, for example, Adam Clayton

Powell, Jr., and the never-to-be-forgotten Father Divine. They might have had harems of boys and girls and monkeys for all we cared: they tried to help us, and they did, and they paid for it.

Black policemen were another matter. We used to say, "If you just *must* call a policeman"—for we hardly ever did—"for God's sake, try to make sure it's a *White* one." A Black policeman could completely demolish you. He knew far more about you than a White policeman could and you were without defenses before this Black brother in uniform whose entire reason for breathing seemed to be his hope to offer proof that, though he was Black, he was not Black like you.

In the case of the Atlanta police force, I remembered when the first Black policemen had been hired in Atlanta—in the late forties—and remembered that they had not, then, been permitted to arrest White people. I supposed that they had acquired this power by now; though, as far as I could see, this power could be exercised only on the poor White (who would not take it meekly), there being virtually no other Whites in what we have come to call the inner city.

Some of the Black Atlanta police force were my guides in very strange territory and I find that I don't, yet, really know how to do justice to their patience. When I tried to compare their situation in Atlanta, now, with the situation I remembered from my youth, in Harlem, I found myself facing a void icier than the mere passage of time. The cops I remembered had known what the community felt about them, and it hadn't seemed to matter. Here, they knew, too, that many elements of the community distrusted them, but the knowledge seemed to sting.

This is due not only to the fact that policemen also have children, it has something to do with the vicissitudes of the Black community, North and South, in time.

I was born in Harlem, in time for the Harlem Renaissance, the Jazz Age, and the Great Depression—all of these preceded by the War to End War. Black soldiers fought in this war, to win monumental and universal honors. No less a figure than W. E. B. Du Bois had proclaimed that never again could the American Republic treat the darker brother as less than a man.

The people who produced me had just, like the Israelites, left Egypt: had yet to sing (eventually accompanied by Du Bois), *Lord, I wish I had of died in Egypt land!*

I was born in 1924. It was not until I started going to school, which would have been, I suppose, around 1929, that I began to be aware of the "Hill." The Hill was Sugar Hill, where well-to-do Negroes lived. I began to be aware of it because many of my teachers lived there. It was not so very far, geographically, from 133rd Street, between Fifth and Lenox avenues, where my family and I lived—but it was a different world. It turned its back on the Harlem River, which ends Harlem on the east, and paraded majestically westward, rising on hills, and seemed to stretch endlessly uptown, farther than the eye could see, into Canaan. The buildings were handsome and spotless, the doormen arrogant and tall. My teachers included the novelist Jesse Huff Fauset, for example, and Countee Cullen—I did not know who they were, yet—and others, less celebrated but part of the same world. Some of my teachers invited me to their homes sometimes for tea and cookies or peanut-butter sandwiches or doughnuts, and I was very grateful, very shy, and thoroughly bewildered. My principal, at P.S. 24, was Mrs. Gertrude Elise Ayer, the only Negro school principal in the New York City public-school system—and, according to Dr. Kenneth Clark, until 1963, anyway, the only one—and, for me, she was a breathtakingly beautiful woman, a *colored* woman.

l was lucky. Mrs. Ayer, and my teachers, Black and White, expected something from me. (Harlem, I repeat, was not an all-Black community then.) I did not know what, exactly, they expected, but a child reacts to the value you place on it. It was rarely said directly to me (though I overheard grown-up conversations) but it was made clear that I could—and, therefore, must—become a great help and credit to my race.

Lord. The words sound, now, so beautifully naïve, so trusting. For we felt, then—or, rather, the people who were handling me felt, then—that we had only to prove our worth and no one could deny our right to live in our country, as free as all other citizens.

I say *we*: but this was the Hill, not the Hollow, still less the factory or the chain gang. Prove *what*? *how*? *to whom*? and, finally, assuming that anything *can* be proven to White Americans—assuming that we have not furnished sufficient proof already—*Why?*

This was certainly the attitude of Marcus Garvey and the people who became a part of the Back to Africa movement—a movement that my father seemed to hold in high esteem. This movement, as we would now say, was "destabilized" and smashed, and Garvey, after serving time in a federal penitentiary, returned, broken, to Jamaica. The official Negro organizations had opposed him, and, as has been suggested, may have helped the American government to break him. Ironically, Du Bois, a Pan-Africanist, was one of Garvey's most implacable foes. Ironically, too—after the Second World War—Du Bois parted company with the NAACP; apparently became a Communist; like the late Paul Robeson and the late Canada Lee, was hounded virtually to extinction by the government he had so trusted; and died in Ghana, at the age of ninety-four, the day before the March on Washington.

In my part of the ghetto, then—in the Hollow—preparing for the new day a-coming, we scrubbed ourselves mercilessly with hard brushes, soap and water, and Vaselined our ashy faces, elbows, hands, and knees and hair. Our clothes, however strikingly improvised, were clean. We minded our manners. We respected our elders. To be called Black was an insult. That word could lead to blows and blood and, even, death.

And yet—none of this altered our situation in any way whatever. When we went downtown, outside the ghetto, we were niggers. No one had any hesitation about letting us know it, and not only in speech. When I began, sometimes, to pick up my mother out of the White lady's kitchen, downtown, I hated that White lady with all my heart, and when I some-times went downtown with my father's union dues in an enve-lope, I hated those filthy, slimy, cigar-smelling White men and longed for the power to kill.

We wanted to be on our way, we were eager. We were ready. But no one else was ready, except with a blow. And, as I began to realize who some of my teachers really were, I began to hear another tone in their swift, good-natured asides to each other—a kind of shorthand, which it was not meant for me to translate—and, with my family, dealing with the hideous results of my father's working day and week, and when I began to hate myself, or, at least, profoundly to doubt my worth, because I was a nigger, I began to understand the Black cop of that time and place. My father worked with White people all day and all week long: that was why he hated them. And I really do not believe that Christ Himself, beseeching, or the threat of eternal damnation, could possibly have eradicated this hatred: my father would have fed on it in Hell. He couldn't reach the White people he hated, he couldn't strike them: so he struck us. And so was the Black cop, for his White co-workers, just another nigger. He couldn't strike them, but he could take it out on us. This self-perpetuating rage and anguish is because the man who wishes to bless is forced to curse, and the hand that would caress is forced to strike.

Though there was a community in Harlem, then, and a real connection between the elders and the young, it was a captive community, destined to be smashed a long, long way from Canaan. Death took the elders. Then, drugs were dumped into the ghetto, to take the young. The Black responsibility for the Black condition is more crucial now, and more visible, than it has ever been before. There are some Whites—there are many—who understand this very well, and welcome it; but they do not form a majority of the White population.

The police spoke very little of Wayne Williams, volunteered no opinions concerning his character, or his guilt. This is, of course, professional responsibility, and I was operating, after all, furthermore, as a journalist, but I was grateful for their silence.

The air was wicked with speculation. One scenario suggested, for example, that the father, Homer Williams, a freelance photographer—whom I must, certainly, therefore, have encountered during my previous journeys to Atlanta—is as failed a man as his son; that the mother never forgave the father for being a failure, nor did the son—listening, allegedly, to the mother. Further, that the father, subsequent to some grim scandal, involving boys, lost his teaching job and, then, sodomized the son, thus giving the son a lethal blackmail power over him, this accounting for their (allegedly) icy relationship—from which gaudy sequence of events, one is to conclude, the Atlanta murders occurred.

Of course, anything is possible and, perhaps, I, too, would love to believe it. It would make it easier to file the case away, and close it. But, though I have never been allowed to meet the son, I have met the father *and* the mother. The fact that the suspension of judgment may be impossible does not release one from the responsibility of perception. And that anything can happen is proven, perhaps, by the mere existence of this vindictive and self-serving legend, designed to destroy and to justify the destruction of three living human beings.

No one in the streets, as far as I could discern, believed it for a moment: it was too brutally and clearly beside the point. For, even if it were true, it is a universal not to say daily event, and has nothing whatever to do with the slaughter of the children of Atlanta.

The cowardice of this time and place—this era—is nowhere more clearly revealed than in the perpetual attempt to make the public and social disaster the result, or the issue, of a single demented creature or, perhaps, half a dozen such creatures, who have, quite incomprehensibly, gone off their rockers and who must be murdered or locked up. Thus, for example, these present days, to describe a person, or group of persons, as *leftists*, *guerrillas*, or *terrorists* is to dismiss their claim to human attention: we are not compelled to think of them at all anymore, except as the vermin that must be destroyed. Or, in another way, but for the same reason, we are still attempting to explain Hitler away: we do not wish to see him in our mirror. Or Franco: who could not have terrorized Spain so long without the support of the "free" world. Or Mobutu, a puppet of the West, one of the people directly responsible for the murder of Lumumba. Being aware of the libel laws, I am not suggesting that they ever sodomized anyone; but, if they had, would anyone in the "free" world care? And, in any case, how can their quaint domestic habits—whatever they may be—account for their ruinous power in the world?

The mother and father pointed out to me—and no one has contested this—that, in spite of the (seeming) wealth of fiber evidence, there were no fingerprints anywhere—not in the house, not on the walls, not in the car. And, though it is claimed that the murderer changed his "pattern" once it was "leaked"—by hostile White policemen, dismissed by the Black Administration—that fiber evidence was being used, and began dumping the bodies in the river, you will have observed that I have had some difficulty locating this "pattern." While I was in Atlanta, bodies were being found in all kinds of places, including the river, and some were decomposing. If the murderer changed his "pattern" upon learning of the probable use of fiber evidence, it would be interesting to know in what time span this discovery occurred since *some* of the bodies *were* found in the river before that famous *splash* on the bridge and some of the bodies were not found for something like a year.

One can live quite well in Atlanta for a fraction of what life costs in New York, and this is true—or was—even for the very poor. The wretched of Atlanta do not, of course, awaken every morning praising God that they are not among the wretched of New York: "comparative" poverty exists only for those who know nothing of poverty. But one can live quite well in Atlanta on far less money than the same "lifestyle" would require in New York. Thus, just as the poor are thrown together, so, though with somewhat more breathing space, are the comparatively well-off. (The Judge and the Williams family live on the same side of town—inevitably, since they are not in the suburbs.) And this means that Atlanta gives the impression of being a hermetic city, sealed and volcanic, containing, it seemed to me, some of the loneliest (and most gallant) people in the world. (I have never seen so many bachelors living alone in houses that, in New York, would be considered mansions; indeed, even in Atlanta, they resemble mansions.)

A city dominated by the middle class is a city dominated by churches and this particular inevitability, in the case of Atlanta, means many things: in a city where so much must be hidden, it is feared, perpetually, that everything is known.

This means that the Terror did not so much alter the climate of Atlanta as reveal, or, as it were, epiphanize it. There's a person going around, indeed, not taking names this time, but children's lives and this person may be anyone you meet. For there was a moment when Atlanta was by no means certain that the murders were being committed by a man.

Or by one man.

For you cannot, it seems to me, quite have it both ways. Either you have a maniac (*son of Satan!*) stalking the city, intimidating or seducing young boys into his (allegedly, and for the most part) green station wagon or you have a member of the community, who manages, also, to spirit away and murder two young girls—one, out of the house where her parents lay sleeping.

The police report does not indicate any evidence of sexual violation: according to the police report, none of the crimes was sexual. Yet, a great deal depends on what one makes of the word, *sexual*—what one supposes *sexual* to mean—for, also, according to the police report, the child's body was stripped and bathed, then, in one way or another (*cause of death!*), murdered and left, in some visible place, to be found.

Everything, anything, is possible. Yet, I find it somewhat beyond the limit of probability that the failed Wayne Williams—somewhat young, after all, to be described as a failure son—of the (possibly) failed Homer Williams, could have been so energetic.

He impresses me as a chubby, weak, arrogant boy: *all* arrogant people are weak. He impresses me, too, in spite of his seeming energy, as a profoundly lazy boy: the key to the despair, never quite hidden, in the faces of his parents. It has been known to happen that arrogant, chubby, weak, and lazy people turn themselves into "talent scouts," which, allegedly, is how Wayne Williams met his victims. But we are not discussing the mortality rate of Hollywood, or Broadway: we are confronted with the bloody events occurring in what is, by contrast or comparison, a very small, sealed town. It can be said that Wayne Williams was being a "talent scout" when, at the age of twelve, or thereabouts, he and his friends interviewed Andrew Young. This interview would have placed them, as we put it, "on the map." For, a "talent scout" is exactly that, a "scout," and he does not, consciously or deliberately, destroy his bread and butter.

It is possible that the younger Williams's vindictiveness is directed against his parents, and is the key to their performance in the courtroom. According to witnesses, they never acknowledged each other, or he, at least, never seemed to recognize them. There can be many reasons for this, an anguished pride being not the least—the refusal to weep, or react at all, in public. It is possible that he blamed his parents, as they had allowed him to do, and that they blamed themselves: as he had always insisted that they should.

And, I suspect, though this is hazardous speculation, that his relationship to his parents, which would seem to be his only real relationship to anyone, is the key to his performances on the witness stand on the first and second day of his testimony. On the first day, he was a "nice" boy, knowing that his parents would do anything for him: they always had. On the second day, he realized that there was nothing they could do. He was on his own. "You want the real Wayne Williams? You got him right here." In terms of the public response (to a presumed mass murderer) the effect of this performance was disastrous. But I agree with the White man who said, bleakly, "If he'd been White, it wouldn't have hurt him."

Much has been made of the fact (assuming it to *be* a fact) that Wayne Williams denied knowing any of the victims, yet was photographed in proximity to some of them—"holding hands" somebody said. This crucial piece of evidence has failed to be as ruthlessly publicized as it should certainly have been. Furthermore, neither the denial nor the holding of hands can prove murder or the intent to murder—to say nothing of the fact that, in Atlanta, proximity to the victims is completely unavoidable. *I* may have been photographed with some of them: they were all over the streets, and they stalked the Omni. The idea of Williams as a talent scout would have spread like fire through the streets of this walled city: children bring the news home. Yet, no one appears to have associated Wayne Williams with the Terror until he was placed under *open surveillance.* It is a lethal legal principle so to mark a man before he is accused of any crime, and, so, to arrest him, and bring him to trial. It is impossible for him to have, as the quaint American jargon puts it, a *fair* trial: he has already been condemned.

There was, also, speculation that Wayne Williams was part of a homosexual ring that seduced, into a certain Atlanta house, young boys. That such houses exist, in Atlanta, as elsewhere, is beyond question; yet, Williams seems a somewhat unlikely recruiter. In any case, the place to which a male child may go for sexual release is not likely to be the place from which he does not return: rumor spreads quickly in the streets. (Quite apart from the fact that the houses are not indispensable: any bus stop or movie-house toilet, or alleyway, will do.) If your friend goes to *The House of the Rising Sun* and does not return, if you never see him alive again, then you will never be able to enter it. It is the awakening of desire, in this somewhat obscene culture, that precipitates guilt, and guilt which precipitates the fear of death. And, sooner or later, the child will tell *somebody*: he need speak only once, and the news is out.

It can be said that the racial terror obscured the private one.

But let us, for a moment, attempt to confront the meaning— the weight—of racial terror. It is important that I try to make you understand that I refuse, absolutely, to speak from the point of view of the victim. The victim can have no point of view for precisely so long as he thinks of himself as a victim. The testimony of the victim, as victim, corroborates, simply, the reality of the chains that bind him—confirms, and, as it were, consoles the jailer, the keeper of the keys. For precisely as long as the jailer hears your moaning, he knows where you are. The sound of the victim's moaning confirms the authority of the jailer, the keeper of the keys: those keys that, designed to lock you out, inexorably lock him in. He is the prisoner of the delusion of his power, to which he has surrendered any possibility of identity, or the private life, and he glimpses this, sometimes, in his mirror, or in the eyes of his children. His only real hope is death. That is why he cannot love his children, the proof being that he dare not consider his dreadful legacy, this fire-bombed earth: his only real achievement.

To realize that one is, oneself, and from the moment of one's birth, both subject and object of the human cowardice—for that is what it is—of what translates itself, in action—the Word made flesh! of racial terror, demands a ruthless cunning, an impenetrable style, and an ability to carry death, like a bluebird, on the shoulder. Thus, when I suggest that, in Atlanta, the racial terror obscured the private one, I am speaking of a reflex, of habit. Thus, inevitably, and especially considering the bloody record of the heirs of Manifest Destiny, Atlanta's first reaction to the murders was to assume that this was an action of the Ku Klux Klan—alive, my friends, and well, and living in the USA. Then, when it began to be clear that this latest pogrom was rooted in our history and demanded Black/Black collaboration, one found oneself standing on a steep height. Our countrymen have never loved us, nor ever, indeed, considered us to be their countrymen. The proof, and I challenge anyone alive to deny it, is in every single American institution, from the schools to the labor unions, to say nothing of the churches, or yesterday's Liberals, the Negro's friends, who have now become the Neoconservatives. My old running buddies, some of whom I trusted, with perfect confidence, with my life.

One may add, for I would like to have this on my record, that the Reagan vote was an anti-Black/Black vote—absolutely—and one may also add (and I would welcome being challenged on this) that less than thirty percent of the American people voted. So much for the "resounding mandate."

I said, the child must tell *someone*; but, apparently, no child did. He may have spoken to his peers. But I spoke to some of the children. Obviously, they would not tell *me*, either, and children can be devastatingly devious. Still, the question of sexual disaster, so vivid in the minds of some of the elders, seemed not to have troubled the minds of the children. When I say "elders" I am not referring to the parents, who were mainly speechless, as was I. Yet, I will remember, until I die, the face of the father of Patrick Balthazar, and the afternoon I spent with him, and his eyes, and his voice, and Camille Bell, and Ms. Hill. Whatever happened in Atlanta has nothing to do with *The House of the Rising Sun*, or *A Streetcar Named Desire*. It has far more to do with *Ghosts*.

I am making a very deliberate effort to make you put two ordeals—the Black and the White—side by side. The real and unanswerable disaster of that history that calls itself White is that, first of all, in the world in which we live, there is no other history. History is a hymn to White people, and all us others have been *discovered*—by White people, who may or may not (they suppose) permit us to enter history. This history can, for example, be said to reach a kind of culmination in the unspeakable and indescribable combination of arrogance and mediocrity that marks those cousins, the English and the German, is contained in their extraordinary assumption that the key to Civilization is in their hands. This is to assume that the summit of human ambition must be to become the Kaiser or citizen of a blood-drenched paranoid territory, or king or queen of a damp and claustrophobic island, inhabited, mainly, by the most notorious victims of the war between the Church and the State and the first orphans created by the Industrial Revolution. Neither the Europeans nor the Americans are able to recognize that they, mercilessly, enslaved each other before they attempted a passage to India, or hoisted sail for Africa. And all that has united Europe, as Europe, or Europe and America, until today, is not the color White but what they perceive as the color Black. They do not care about each other at all, never have, and it is inconceivable that they ever will. The English treat the Irish and the Scottish, for example, like dogs, and they treat each other the same way: to open your mouth in England is hazardous, your accent revealing your origins, and, therefore, your human value. The Europeans never dreamed of a Common Market until it was conceived as a means of maintaining slavery, and, even under that pressure, were quite unable to cease arguing over tariffs, borders, wine, sheep, and automobiles, and never dreamed of buying a Japanese patent exactly as they would have bought any European patent, because the Japanese are not "civilized." And the West quite fails to see the unforgivable enormity of Hiroshima—repeat: unforgivable—nor, since it believes in a history that is entirely its invention, does it have any sense of the dreadful tenacity of human memory, what that memory records, and how every bill must be paid. Speaking as a creation of the ancestral memory—otherwise, neither I nor any other Black American would be breathing—I can tell you not only that my soul is a witness, but that what goes around, comes around. A people who trust their history do not find themselves immobilized in it. The Western world is located somewhere between the Statue of Liberty and the pillar of salt.

At the center of the European horror is their religion: a religion by which it is intended one be coerced, and in which no one believes, the proof being the Black/White conditions, or options, the horror into which the cowardly delusion of White Supremacy seems to have transformed Africa, and the utterly intolerable nightmare of the American Dream. I speak with the authority of the grandson of a slave, issue of the bondswoman, Hagar's child. And, what the slave did—despised and rejected, *'buked and scorned*—with the European's paranoid vision of human life was to alchemize it into a force that contained a human use. The Black preacher, since the church was the only Civilized institution that we were permitted—separately—to enter, was our first warrior, *terrorist*, or *guerrilla. He* said that freedom was real—that *we* were real. *He* told us that *trouble don't last always. He* told us that our children and our elders were sacred, when the Civilized were spitting on them and hacking them to pieces, in the name of God, and in order to keep on making money. And, furthermore, we were not so much permitted to *enter* the church as corralled into it, as a means of rendering us docile and as a means of forcing us to corroborate the inscrutable will of God, Who had decreed that we should be slaves forever.

What a cowardly, not to say despicable, vision of human life; what a dreadful concept of divinity! Yet, what the Blacks achieved—and it cannot, now, be undone, except by blowing up the universe, which the Civilized world is quite cowardly enough to do—was to dig through the rubble, in Africa, in the Caribbean, and in North America, to find their ancestors, their gods, and themselves. There are many gods, not One: and, if there were One, He would not be White. This is really the news we are receiving from what we call Islam, from the stammering Pope, the Bank of the Holy Ghost, and Chase Manhattan, and Soweto, and Jehovah's most notorious client-state, Israel, thoughtfully underwritten, however, by Western capital—more than we can say for Harlem: which brings us back to Atlanta.

The Black man's first encounter with the West—by which I mean, mainly, the Christian church—brought him devastation and death, we are only, now, beginning to recover, are beginning, out of the most momentous diaspora in human memory, to rediscover and recognize each other. This is a global matter, and the denouement of this encounter will be bloody and severe: precisely because it demolishes the morality, to say nothing of the definitions, of the Western world. It is by no means amusing to realize that my nephew, for example, may be called upon to liberate El Salvador—or Poland—long before he can set foot in South Africa. Yet, my nephew will live to see the year 2000, when he will be about thirty years younger than I am now, and the present kings and queens of England (for example) will be feasting on milk and honey—a typically indigestible English diet—and leading choirs in song at an eternal banquet at which, thank our ancestors!, his presence will not be required.

The White man, someone told me, *discovered the Cross by way of the Bible, but the Black man discovered the Bible by way of the Cross.*

This has something to do with the style and the anguish of the Atlanta confrontation. This has something to do, in fact, with being civilized: to be civilized demands that one recognize and respect the human journey, the long march or the short walk. Whoever cannot do this—cannot, for example, treat every child as sacred—cannot believe in God, or in any gods whatever. He/she believes in safety, that delusion which is death-in-life and which permits, indeed compels, my unhappy countrymen—who do not dare think of themselves as other than White, and who, therefore, cannot think of me as other than Black, or, at best, their doomed or fortunate imitation—to have inherited Spain's title: *The Nation with the Bloody Footprint.*

The paradox of what we react to as the American Dream *and* as the American dilemma is that it is a space—it is certainly not yet a nation, whatever that concept may come, in time, to mean—ruled by Whites and dominated by Blacks.

Washington, the "American" capital, is known as *Chocolate City.* It is, perhaps, the very definition of the *inner* city, the Blacks being entirely encircled by the Whites—the reverse image, but the very same principle as that of the wagon train, in which, you will remember, the Civilized formed themselves into a circle closing the Heathen out—or, perhaps more accurately, and more nearly contemporary, a kind of latter-day Congo Square, that space in which the slaves were allowed to worship under the eyes and the guns of their masters.

Like almost all Black American events it was somewhat underrated, and, yet, it is worth pointing out that the Watergate "scandal" was precipitated by a Black porter, who was the only noncriminal in this sordid affair, and who was merely doing his duty. Unlike the White criminals, he never made—out of the execution of his duty—a single TV show, book, dime, or pulpit: he failed, quite, to recognize that it was necessary to be born again. Neither the exiting nor the entering president so much as patted him on the head, or dreamed of offering him any recompense. Yet, it was he who blew the whistle that turned a global spotlight not only on criminals but on the curious state of affairs in this curious and crucial country.

And, in a way not, after all, dissimilar—since mothers can

assume that they have duties toward their issue, whether that issue be present or absent, male or female, living or dead—it was a Black woman, Ms. Camille Bell, who blew the whistle in Atlanta.

That whistle forced Authority to enter, control, and close a case concerning slaughtered Black children, most of them males, a banality with which (and I am a witness) they had never, previously, been remotely concerned.

On the contrary: never, in all my years on earth, have I expected White power, willingly, to protect my Black life, though those in power have sometimes found themselves coerced— for reasons of their own—into doing so. (*White power* is to be distinguished from people who happen to have been born, as we put it, White, and I owe my life to some of those people. The world's definitions are one thing and the life one actually lives is quite another. One cannot allow oneself, nor can one's family, friends, or lovers—to say nothing of one's children—to live according to the world's definitions: one must find a way, perpetually, to be stronger and better than that.)

I was not in Atlanta when Dick Gregory spoke, but I think I can describe us as friends and we saw each other when I came in. Now is not the moment for me to attempt a sketch of Gregory. I may not know him well, but I have known him a very long time, and I admire and respect him very much. He can be accused, perhaps, of an excess of intensity—though this accusation is almost always hurled by people incapable of any intensity at all—but it is very rare that one is privileged, even from a distance, to watch a man transform himself from within, and pay the silent price for that.

That man has a certain radiance—that is to say, a certain authority. That one may agree or disagree with him is not important. One listens because, whatever he is doing, he is not lying, and one of you may be wrong.

Or both of you—with a man like Gregory, you can pursue the conundrum. Anyway, he had upset Atlanta, or many people in Atlanta. He had suggested (it was not, as I was allowed to assume, at the pressure of an *accusation*) that the key to the Terror was in the nature of a scientific experiment. I am being very deliberately vague, but the nature of the experiment was based on the possibility that the tip of the Black male sexual organ contained a substance that might be used to cure cancer.

People found this an appalling suggestion. I did not. I wondered why they did. It was during my lifetime, after all, and in my country, somewhere in a prison in the "American" South, that Black men with syphilis were allowed to die, while being scrutinized. What scientific strides were made because of this experiment I do not know, but the experiment was made. And who, in a Republic noted, after all, and indisputably, for the energy of the genocidal will—Manifest Destiny!—can, and with what authority come forward to assure that remnant called the American people, and especially me and Uncas, that our lives are now held so sacred that such an experiment is unthinkable?

I tend to doubt Dick's suggestion because—apart from the fact that I *want* to doubt it—it seems such an untidy way of carrying on a scientific experiment. But, then, one is forced to realize that a scientific experiment *must* be untidy: that is why it is called an experiment.

I have mentioned a city dominated by churches, which brings me before the decidedly disagreeable necessity of attempting to suggest something of the nature of the dilemma in which the family of the late Dr. Martin Luther King, Jr., live. If I had my way, I would not mention the King family at all. I care too much, if I may say so, about this family, have too deep a respect for their ordeal, and they could live, I am sure, beyond doomsday, without having another word written about them.

But the situation of this family has something to tell us about the Black American journey and the nature of our present confrontation, or crossroad.

There is really nothing to be said concerning the late M. L. King, Sr., who arrived as a youth in Atlanta, in 1916, and, by means of trials neither Horatio Alger nor Ronald Reagan is even remotely equipped to imagine, created a family *and* a church, to lose two sons, and a wife, in a roar of bullets and veil of blood—at the hands of his countrymen. Nor is there anything to be said concerning the most visible of the widows. It is, simply, none of our business.

At the risk of belaboring the obvious—which may not, however, be possible in the narcotized vacuum that North America has become—I would like to point out that Martin Luther King, Jr., for the people whom he loved and served, was not a (pious) martyr. We, the Blacks, have not confused him with Washington, Jefferson, or Abraham Lincoln; we have lived with that inheritance for a while. Nor was he a *victim*. He was not even a *hero*. These terms are meant to distract one from, and, as it were, justify the obscenity of the publicly and privately willed event that transformed him into a *corpse*. No more than the slaughter of Medgar Evers can be charged to a lone(!) lunatic in Mississippi, can Martin's death be set down at the threshold of one deranged, unhappy cowboy. Martin is dead because he was our *witness*—still is, for that matter. That is why he was put to death. For he was *put to death*—he was *assassinated*—by the cowardice of the American people and the will of those who control whatever can be said to remain of the American Republic.

Mrs. King put on my wrist the only watch I have not lost, or broken. Martin's face is on this watch, and the words *I have a dream.*

I have a dream. Ebenezer Baptist is not very far from the Martin Luther King, Jr., Center for Social Change. I have walked it more than a few times. I visited Hosea Williams, at his headquarters, and went to Ralph David Abernathy's church, and spent some time with Andrew Young. Ebenezer was my focal point, in Atlanta, twenty-eight years ago, when I was thirty-three, and when the men I have named (who were my guides) were younger. And, in Alabama, I saw Reverend Shuttlesworth, and sat down beside him in the Montgomery courthouse where a certain J. B. Stoner was "on trial" for having been responsible for at least two of the fifty unsolved bombings in Alabama alone in that year, nearly a quarter of a century ago, one of them being the bombing of Shuttlesworth's church, and home—that year, that distant year, when the Reverend Shuttlesworth and his wife were nearly murdered in the streets of Alabama by the law enforcers, when four Black girls were bombed out of a Sunday school into eternity, and when dogs and horses were turned on children by the guardians of Civilization and the leaders of the "free" world. Shuttlesworth was also my guide. I had never been south before—that year, that distant year. *If they'd brought somebody to trial*, then, said Shuttlesworth, *it might have made a difference. It makes no difference now.* Stoner had many friends in the courtroom, and he and the Judge were very friendly with each other. I do not have the stamina to describe the "trial": Stoner received a ten-year suspended sentence, which is to say that he walked out as free as lightning. Shuttlesworth and I said not a word to each other during this indescribably obscene mockery of whatever it may mean to attempt to become a human being and hope to be equal to human responsibility. On the other hand, it will, no doubt, relieve my countrymen to be informed that this was, in fact, and in Alabama!, a desegregated courtroom. Fred Shuttlesworth and I were sitting next to, not to say were surrounded by, exceedingly cheerful White men who menaced us with not the faintest scowl and who wore their Ku Klux Klan insignia on the sidebars of their eyeglasses.

I have a dream. This dream must, alas, be disentangled from whatever nightmare controls this fearfully White Republic. Difficult it is to make bricks without straw. We may be doomed to discover that it is not impossible; we may, indeed, be on the edge of the recognition that making bricks without straw is, precisely, our historical and actual specialty. Who, after all, has ever given the Black people of this country anything? Certainly not forty acres and a mule. Certainly not the right to love and be responsible for our men and our women and our children. Certainly not the right to learn and to act on what we learn. Certainly not the right to repudiate the imposed model and create, and act, on our own—no: it has always been assumed that the Black's only possible aspiration would be to become White. Which is a curiously loaded conundrum when one considers how many White multitudes found, and find, themselves in Africa because they were bored with being White and hoped to become Black, as it were, painlessly, and without laying down what Kipling called "the White Man's burden." Or, in other words, although White people don't wish to be White (*cf. the beat generation!*), it is very important for White people that

Black people should wish to be White. England and France, for example, to name two localities, are wretched with furiously embittered people who will never recover from having been forced to leave Algeria, or Kenya, for example, from having been rejected by a people they claim to despise. And they did, and do, despise them, of course; it was necessary in order to justify—sanctify—the uses to which these humans were put. This is a decidedly terrifying view of one's own humanity and the possibilities of human life. This civilization has proven itself capable of destroying peoples rather than hear them, destroying continents rather than share them, and are capable, for the same reason, of destroying all life on this planet.

This will not happen. But a dreadful day is upon us, and, as nobody's going to give us any straw—Ireland was raped, and the Irish were allowed to starve *to death*, in order to protect the profits of British merchants—people, we best make ourselves ready.

I have a dream. Ebenezer and the M. L. King, Jr., Center are, as I have said, within walking distance of each other. The Center is a monument, and so is Ebenezer: the Center comes out of the passion that created Ebenezer. Bricks without straw: there was no phone connecting us to the White House but there was a rumor controlling us from the streets. Bricks without straw: people who are neither whores nor fools (I am speaking of Black people) opted for the present Administration in the hope of getting a little straw. God knows that I am not trying to minimize the anguish. But if there is no straw in that stable for the South African miner—to use, simply, the most vividly indefensible example—then there can be no straw for us—or, such straw as may have been hoarded (after having been, in fact, extorted) will be used to bribe the natives of the Caribbean into becoming the new niggers of the New World.

That, in fact, will not work, either, the hour is too late, the facts too blatant, and there *is* no straw.

Or, put it another way: we, the Blacks, the North American Blacks, who were capable of producing other crops and desperate to feed our children, were forced to produce a *cash* crop: cotton. The institution (the peculiar institution!) of slavery, which might, otherwise, have ceased to be profitable, was saved by Eli Whitney's invention of the cotton gin. This did not make the slave's work easier, which was, in any case, not the point, but it made it faster: if one excepts the Pyramids, it was probably the world's most momentous assembly line. The people who picked the cotton and who sold it, at prices dictated by others, also eventually bought their manufactured products back, as a wedding gown, or a shirt, or a shroud, at prices dictated by others. Just as the Cubans, who may have preferred growing corn or sweet potatoes, were forced to turn their entire island into a sugar-producing plantation—the cash crop!—which sugar they sold to the "free" world at prices dictated by the Free World, and then bought back, a year later, at prices dictated by the Free World. Now we are deciding to boycott Nicaraguan sugar—in order to save the natives from communism—and, for the very same reason, exhibiting the same unshakable nobility of purpose, do not dream of boycotting anything produced by the South African economy, an economy based on slavery. On Black slavery.

We, the American Blacks, then, are expected to imagine that a Republic that has not been able, after something like four hundred years, to imagine or deliver our freedom, here, will, somehow, cajole South Africa into letting our people go. The Republic can bring ruinous pressure to bear on Central America (*mare nostrum!*) but the Black South African slave will simply have to wait—as we have. Until the hour that the sweat of his brow—the delivery of the cash crop—is no longer needed and he can be dispatched, discreetly or otherwise, to his ancestors.

For *that* is, really, the American Dream. The doctrine of White Supremacy—which, in America, translated itself into the doctrine of Manifest Destiny, having returned to Europe, and, like a plague carried by the wind, infests all the cities of Europe—is all that now unites the so-called Old World with the so-called New.

This places the Afro-American in a stunning and vertiginous place.

Immediately upon the verdict, Lee Brown, the Police Commissioner, one of my guides in Atlanta, and a very winning man, closed the case (leaving, however, seven other cases "unsolved") and moved to Houston, Texas, to become Police Commissioner there.

Rather like the Governor's meeting, at which so many people assured me they had not been present that I realized that it must have occurred, the departure of the Police Commissioner, already, after all, sufficiently striking, began to press on my mind because so many people were anxious to explain it to me. Every state in the Union had been after Police Commissioner Brown, nor do I doubt that this is true. He would not leave Atlanta until the case was closed. I do not doubt that, either; though when I was forced to think about it, I realized that it would have been virtually impossible for him to have left Atlanta—at least, to take another post—before this case was closed. To have left Atlanta *before* this case was closed might very well have resulted in the ruin of his career. It would certainly have compromised his credibility in the Black community and diminished his possible usefulness to the White Republic: for the one depends on the other—the dimensions, precisely, of the trap. Or, to switch metaphors, the tension of the tightrope.

In any case, he had turned down every offer until the phone from Houston rang, and accepted it, according to one of my informants, because somebody made the right phone call, at the right time.

I did not, as I say, really think about this until I was forced to think about it. When I began to think about it, I realized that I had been doing what every writer, unconsciously, is always doing: a writer is never listening to what is being said, he is never listening to what he is being told. He is listening to what is *not* being said, he is listening to what he is *not* being told, which means that he is trying to discover the purpose of the communication.

As far as I was concerned, Lee Brown was an indisputably honorable, even gallant, man, confronting an enormity, and it had not occurred to me that he needed to be defended.

Then, I realized that it was not *he* who was being defended, but the case itself, and the verdict, and he was moved on up, and, above all, out.

Fingerprint evidence appears to be one of the many Oriental contributions to the West, first being heard of, as far as I have been able to discover, in Persia, in the fifteenth century, and, then, at the University of Bologna, in the seventeenth century. It had come to British attention by 1858, in India, and, by 1877, a certain Dr. H. Fowles used fingerprint evidence, in Tokyo. It appears to have entered the United States in 1882, by means of a certain Gilbert Thompson, and, by 1883, Mark

Twain is writing about fingerprint evidence, in *Life on the Mississippi*, and in *Pudd'nhead Wilson*. Someone named Francis Galton has written a book about fingerprint evidence by 1893. It was first used in a murder case in La Plata, Argentina, in 1892, and was first used in a murder case in the United States in 1924, in Leavenworth, when two Black men, Will West and William West, who not only answered to the same names, but who looked, apparently, exactly alike, were distinguished from each other by means of fingerprints.

There is something alarming about this decidedly imperial history, moving, as it were, from dark to black, and suggesting something in the nature of an experiment with or on the natives. Fingerprint evidence has, by now, in any case, become so completely unquestionable that the Williams family cites the lack of fingerprint evidence as proof of the innocence of their son.

A happily married friend of mine recounts his discovery of fiber evidence.

A friend of the family, a red-haired woman, came to visit, and, during her visit, took a bath. She, then, went on her way. Subsequently, my friend took a bath. As his wife was helping him, or watching him, dress, she noticed one or two red hairs in the hair on his chest. (My friend has hair on his chest.) Well, she didn't know how it got there, and *he* didn't know how it got there, but they finally realized that it must have been a leftover from the hygienic red-haired woman. Some of her hair was still in the tub when my friend took his bath. They did not have a quarrel or decide to be divorced. The vagrant red hair did not prove that my friend had slept with the lady or taken a bath with her or, even, ogled her in the soapsuds; it proved only that, at some indeterminable point, they had been in the same bathtub—or, if you like, environment. It did not, and it could not, prove that they had ever seen each other. It certainly did not prove—could not prove—that they had ever made love to each other—though my friend's wife, were we discussing a more ordinary American couple, could have used this single red hair in a suit for divorce, and won the case.

The eye of the beholder.

There were seven hundred pieces of fiber evidence used to prove that Wayne Williams was guilty of an indeterminate number of murders, which strikes me as a ruthless bludgeoning of the People, represented by the jury. If we take the official count of thirty corpses, we must subtract the seven cases closed: the seven murders, that is, for which no one will ever be accused. That leaves twenty-three. But Wayne Williams was arrested on the basis of *two* murders—having been, it is worth pointing out, already placed under open surveillance, an interesting legal precedent and a violation of privacy to which it is unlikely that any White citizen of North America would have been exposed—and, then, tried for twenty-eight murders of which he had not been accused. He could be tried for murders of which he had not been accused because the Judge allowed the principle of "prior acts" to control the trial, thus establishing the "pattern" designed to prove Wayne Williams "capable" of murder. This pattern could not prove his guilt: hence, the seven hundred pieces of scientific evidence.

A People who can believe that Ethel and Julius Rosenberg coerced David Greenglass into stealing the secret of the atomic bomb from Los Alamos, thus allowing the Rosenbergs to sell this "secret" to the Russians—and who sent them to the electric chair for this "treason"—are poorly equipped to examine scientific evidence, or, indeed, any evidence at all.

None of the jurors would speak to me—which I think I understand—but the jury consisted of a cunning arrangement of eight Whites and four Blacks—mostly women, which may or may not be a cunning arrangement—in any case, according to a friend: "When Blacks are outnumbered, they (the jury's Blacks) stand up because they think you are menaced. But if this is not so, and they think you've done wrong, they'll send you up."

Indeed.

In any case, the inventory: Wayne Williams was arrested for the murder of two grown men. Once he was placed on trial for these two murders (*if* they were murders) he was *accused* of twenty-eight murders (of children) and, once he was condemned to prison, for life, seven cases were closed, leaving him guilty, then, of twenty-one murders: murders for which he was not arrested.

This is untidy. It also establishes a precedent, a precedent that may lead us, with our consent, to the barbed wire and the gas oven.

Now, to repeat myself, anything is possible, and the man may be guilty, but I smell a rat; and it is impossible to claim that his guilt has been proven, any more than it can be proven that the murders have ceased. For one thing, murder never ceases, and it is absolutely meaningless to say that there have been no murders that "fit the pattern." What pattern? In Georgia?

Some years ago, after the disappearance of civil rights workers Chaney, Goodman, and Schwerner in Mississippi, some friends of mine were dragging the river for their bodies. This one wasn't Schwerner. This one wasn't Goodman. This one wasn't Chaney. Then, as Dave Dennis tells it, "It suddenly struck us—what difference did it make that it wasn't *them*? *What are these bodies doing in the river?*"

That was nineteen years ago. The question has not been answered, and I dare you to go digging in the bayou.

There is a chilling subtext to *render unto Caesar*.

It is not, for example, true that the Jews killed Christ, but they surrendered him to Rome. As they were ruled by a State that the man from Galilee so profoundly disturbed, it seemed easier, on the whole, to collaborate with the State. And that generations unimaginable and unborn pay, down the ages, for this abdication is proven, for but one example, by the state of our inherited Jerusalem—in which no John, these present days, can make himself ready to walk.

Nor can Yusef or Mary: and what good thing, these present days, comes out of Nazareth?

Black people did not invent the legend of color, but only Black people can destroy it, Blacks being the only people who do not need it.

One of the reasons—the principal reason—that this is so, it would seem to me, is that the definition of people in terms of color is humanly impossible. *Humanly* does not refer to the virtues but the possibilities, or limits, of the human being. People can be defined by their color only by the beholder, who, in order to arrive at this definition, must will himself/herself blind. And this is absolutely true: there is not a racist alive who is not a liar and a coward, the proof being that they imagine reality to be at the mercy of their will—or, rather, of their terror. I remember a very celebrated American patriot, for example, proud issue of Yale, who, after a somewhat stormy TV interview on which we had both appeared, upon discovering one of my brothers and myself and a friend in the elevator, hurried, with his friends, down the stairs. He will say, of course, if challenged, that the elevator was crowded, but I remember the split second—the twinkling of an eye—in which he looked at me and he saw me looking at him. Okay. But *I* would have got on the elevator.

The concept of color as a human reality, as a quantity defining the person and sealing that person's fate, is only beginning, at this late hour, to penetrate Guadeloupe, say, or Senegal, having been brought there by bankers and missionaries. It becomes clear—for some—that the more closely one resembles the invader, the more comfortable one's life may become. And, even at that, the question has far less to do with Color/color than it has to do with Civilization/civilization: to be born in the colonies cited is to be taught that one is French. But one is really controlled and identified by one's father and mother: by one's ancestors. The question of color as identity erupts when one arrives on the mainland—where one is not French, where one becomes, and with no warning, a worthless nigger, a thing—less than a thing, a thing containing after all, the potential of honorable use.

It is a curiously loaded fact, but one I think worth pointing out, that even—or especially—in South Africa, the tribal identity is far more crucial than nuances of color. In this, paradoxically, may be found the root of the South African hope, since tribes can make peace but delusions can make only war. And it is time to realize that Europe—the West—which, out of an unspeakable poverty, created the delusion of color, has always depended on Black tribal divisions in order to *divide and rule!* In this endeavor, they have quite overlooked and forgotten the juggernaut of *their* tribal divisions, and nothing is more dangerous than to have one's history, relentlessly pursuing, at one's back. Georgia began as a convict colony and all the waste and terror and hope of love and life and joy and fear of death and dreams of everlasting life were loaded onto that beast of burden, the Black—*the eye of the beholder!*—and, in that dark face, that warm and inescapable presence, the orphan of the Old World saw, every hour of every day, all that he longed to be and hoped that he would never become. For to dare to hope to *become*—to dare to trust the changing light—is to surrender the dream of safety. It means doing one's utmost not to hide from the question perpetually in the eyes of one's lovers or one's children. It means accepting that those who love you (and those who do not love you) see you far better than you will ever see yourself. It means accepting the terms of the contract that you signed at birth, the master copy of which contract is in the vaults of Death. These ruthless terms, it seems to me, make love and life and freedom real: whoever fears to die also fears to live. Whoever fears to die also imagines—*must* imagine—that another can die in his place; hence, the compulsive hacking off of the Black/black man's sex, and the enforced sterilization of Black/black women. The dream of safety can reach culmination or climax only in the nightmare orgasm of genocide.

Don't take my word, children, but check out your sheets as soon as you get them back from Mr. Clean. Mr. Clean's antecedents include Thomas Jefferson and Tarzan, and he is cousin to our presidents. If you have not yet bleached the sheets delivered to you from Korea and Vietnam, call on Mr. Clean to bleach the laundry you are beginning to receive from, for example, El Salvador, give him a raise and have him make himself ready to wash the bloody sheets already on their way to you from Brazil, Argentina, and Mexico—and Miami, and Haiti, and Soweto, and Harlem, and Chicago, and Tallahassee, and Philadelphia, and Boston, and Memphis, and St. Louis, and Newark, and Jackson, and New Orleans, and Birmingham, and Selma, and Natchez, and Nashville, and Los Angeles, and San Francisco, and Oakland, to say nothing of Havana—to say nothing, for that matter, of what was once called Leopoldville, or what was once called Rhodesia. Cecil Rhodes, for whom Rhodesia was named, was Mr. Clean's direct ancestor, which probably explains, if anything can, the fearful energy he expended cleaning up the kitchens of this unimaginably dirty world.

Mr. Clean assumes that you *have* a kitchen, in which you have nothing better to do than listen to him. Mr. Clean assumes that you would be quite unable to keep yourself or your loved ones clean without his stunning and entirely muscular virility. Mr. Clean arrives, flexing them muscles and grinning that grin, to deliver you from the disaster of your filth—which, he charitably concedes, is not your fault. You just don't know no better—don't know what he knows. Just give him a cocaine, or a missile flash or *rush*, and he will clean it up for you in no time at all, and—you can pay later.

You will, certainly, however, pay—for his expertise. For what this species of foreign-aid expert does not want you to begin to suspect is that the shoe, if shoes there are, is on the other foot. We don't need Mr. Clean: nobody, in the entire world, needs Mr. Clean. We, the wretched of Mr. Clean's earth, have been scrubbing kitchens—to leave it at that—for generations, out of the depthless endeavor called love. That is what kept ourselves, and our children, clean. Foreign aid, like all the Great Society programs, means only that Mr. Clean has got to dump on somebody, for money, somewhere, all those abominations he is forced to create. And why? For money. And, when we stop buying, baby, not we, but he, goes under.

The world can live without yet another television commercial, anywhere. The TV commercial, designed, at considerable expense, to persuade you that your (purchased) aroma or your (purchased) jeans, or your (purchased) hair or your (purchased) wine or your (purchased) Scotch or Canada Dry or bourbon, or your (purchased) Jaguar or your (indisputably purchased) diamond, to say nothing of your (purchased) toothpaste, chewing gum, beer, wine, or toilet paper—designed to make you believe that these purchases will make you an irresistibly sexual creature—is the very root and branch of what this desperately dirty-minded Republic means when it talks of pornography. Advertising *is* pornography. But no one is about to attack a billion-dollar business, because (to lift out of context Woody Allen's very moving coda) they need the eggs.

Well. To need the eggs is one condition. To be compelled to attempt to make bricks without straw is another, and it would seem that the two conditions do not easily translate, each to the other. It is one thing to have something to save. It is quite another matter—another reality, altogether—to be forced to recognize that one has nothing to lose.

The confrontation between that person who must believe that there is something to be salvaged and that person who has been compelled to act on the assumption that he has nothing to lose, is the root and branch of the dilemma of this White Republic. It is ironical—I scarcely dare say savagely so. That man who knows he has nothing to lose runs the risk, it is quite true, of coming to a dreadful end; but, by the time he comes to realize this, the turning point is far behind him and there is nothing he can do about it, even if he would.

It is ironical in that his life begins to belong to him, for the first time—because he realizes that it is not his—and, so far from becoming what the European vocabulary would describe as a pessimist, he finds himself nourished by the knowledge that the children must be fed. He realizes that a child cannot be fooled: to lie to a child is to betray the child. In the voices of the children, he hears his ancestors: *Keep your hand on the plow. Hold on.*

Now, however, and precisely for the sake of the children, let us attempt to reconsider the foregoing from another, and contradictory, point of view.

The State has failed, certainly, to prove Wayne Williams guilty. But this archaic incompetence cannot be said to prove him innocent. For the State, his guilt or innocence is a matter of convenience, but, for us, this question—involving, as it does, complicity—must be more urgent and more personal. Wayne Williams is certainly the creation and the object of a racist civilization, culture, history, and State, but so is Andrew Young, and it is absolutely crucial that we begin to choose our victims—to say nothing of our witnesses—for ourselves.

This cannot be done by surrendering to the State's manipulation of the delusion of color. We cannot allow ourselves to be engulfed by the delusion that has brought the Civilization which defines itself as White to such an abject place.

To scrutinize the performance of the Prosecution is not, for example, enough to absolve the Defense. It is perfectly true that the Defense was crippled at the outset by the fact that the entire case depended on the principle of prior acts; without the introduction of this principle, there could have been, simply, no case at all. A trap, however, differs from the marriage bed: there are no conjugal rights or duties and it is impossible to strike a compromise within, or with, a trap.

The Defense allowed the Prosecution to force the accused to answer questions that should never have been asked: *Are you homosexual? Did you ever strike your father?* One fiber-evidence witness (from Dupont) bore witness (testified) for three hours, without an objection, or, apparently, a question—this according to one of the lawyers involved in the case. I do not doubt this, for if the case could be brought to trial only on the basis of the principle of prior acts, the outcome of the case depended entirely on the weight of the fiber evidence. (One wonders what the courtroom must have been like the first time fingerprint evidence was ever used, and then one realizes that one has never even remotely questioned the validity of fingerprint evidence—concerning which, I, for example, know absolutely nothing.)

This dubious case focuses, crucially, on the question of the date of the purchase of the green carpet in the Williams home, the fibers of which apparently became lethally ubiquitous.

Mrs. Williams first testified that the carpet had been bought in 1968, and then said that she was in error: it had been bought in 1971. Both she and Mr. Williams insisted that the later date was the valid one and claimed to have a receipt to prove it. This receipt seems never to have surfaced during the trial, and the receipt that *was*, apparently, used to prove that the carpet was purchased in 1968 was, actually, a receipt for an air conditioner, according, that is, to Mr. and Mrs. Williams. The date of the purchase of the carpet is crucial because, if I have understood the evidence, this particular carpet was not on the market in 1968.

This question is still left hanging, at least as far as Faye and Homer (and Wayne) Williams are concerned. And, though it is probably safe to suppose them capable of perjury in order to save their son, it is also worth pointing out that they do not, necessarily, feel any compulsion to tell the truth to a Republic that has told them nothing but lies. (Certainly I, for example, do not, and liars can never hear the truth. *I* try to tell the truth because it is simpler and more sanitary—and infinitely less calisthenic—than trying to remember where you said you were last night.)

And this Republic has, indeed, told itself and Black people nothing but lies, which is the very definition of the betrayal of the social contract. Therefore, before I could begin to deal with the question of whether or not Faye and Homer Williams were lying, I had to remember that a State, that, for example, could kidnap Morton Sobell out of Mexico, disguising it as a deportation, and slaughter the Rosenbergs by insisting that a table bought from Macy's was actually a gift from the Russians; a State really capable of believing that men, women, and children, one day ahead of death by starvation, constitute a "Communist" menace; a State absolutely, compulsively, determined to destroy all those dark wretched whom they cannot buy, or use, and that murders so many people, daily, domestically, and globally, and *in the name of freedom!*—yes, this State is quite capable of railroading a man to prison, and to death, by means of a false document. It would all be in the day's unexceptional work.

A photograph, presumably taken by Homer Williams, who is, as I have said, a freelance photographer, was offered, to prove the date of purchase of the contested green carpet. This is a photograph of the Williamses' living room. In this photograph, the carpet is beige or brown and Homer Williams claims that this is because he used the wrong filter, which seems fair enough: people understand as much about filters as they do about fibers.

"But, you know," someone said to me, "something in that picture which wasn't brown? Which was *green*? The Christmas tree."

And, while the Defense should certainly have found a way to protect the accused from such lethally leading questions as *Did you ever strike your father?* it, in fact, appears, from the testimony of the neighbors and of anyone who knew the family (who appear to have few intimates) that Wayne ruthlessly tyrannized his parents and that they quarreled loudly all the time. Since his parents called him, from the time he was born, "the miracle child" and went into bankruptcy in order to prove the depth of their faith in him, this is not hard to believe.

And this makes it difficult to dismiss the testimony of the parking-lot attendant who swears that he heard Wayne Williams curse his father and saw Wayne Williams strike him.

And, from absolutely all accounts, the demeanor of the family—father, mother, son—was, in the courtroom, icy. "He did not look at them. They did not look at him. *Nothing* happened between them."

And, though, conceivably, the Defense should have found way to have prevented the question of homosexuality from being raised at all—neither the crimes for which Wayne Williams had been arrested nor the crimes with which these two crimes "linked" him were classed as sexual crimes—it did not help to have a girl testify *before* the trial that she and Wayne Williams had never been lovers. Subsequently, during the trial, she testified that they *had* been lovers—and, then, in a cloud, as it were, of fibers, she disappears.

Nor does one know *what* to make of the testimony of the young male who claims to have been in Wayne's car, unzipping his trousers, at Wayne's request. The moment the boy unzips his trousers, willingly or docilely enough—there being, in this testimony, as I gather, no hint of menace—Wayne remembers that he must get something from the trunk of his car—nylon cord? another breathing boy?—whereupon, in any case, the unzipped boy zips up and zaps out.

One feels trapped in the slave quarters of the Southern gothic romance—other voices, other rooms—and, perhaps, in truth, one is. The Williams trial was occurring in the aftermath, the pounding surf, of a recent double rape, in Decatur: two Black men had raped two White women, without, however, penetrating their White sex or contaminating the Black phallus. They penetrated the women with tree stumps and one of the women died with a Black foot in her face and, then, on her chest. There had been other slaughters, in Columbus, Georgia—none, however, you will be relieved to hear, that "fit the pattern"—and there was, allegedly, a veiled threat, from Slaton, to connect Wayne Williams with these.

There had to have been a whole lot of sweating going on in that courtroom, and not only on the witness stand. *Legality*, according to an Atlanta lawyer I know, *is whatever you say is legal. Common law is what everyone* agrees *is legal.* An appeal will be granted or not granted, depending on whether or not the Court has committed a legal error—on whether or not the Court can be challenged on a legal technicality. The fate of an appeal has nothing to do with the questions of innocence or guilt.

There could scarcely ever have been a case more relentlessly technical. For if you did not believe the fiber evidence, it was impossible to be persuaded of Wayne's guilt. "The fiber evidence got me over the hurdle," someone told me, and, "That jury held hands and cried and prayed—prayed that they would be guided to the right verdict."

I don't doubt it, and they were not alone.

In the wings, awaiting the verdict, was the question of the future, or demise, of the Special Task Force, as well as the probability that the ubiquitous and indefinable "pattern" would be challenged. The death of Edward Hope Smith, for example, was "linked" to the "pattern," whereas the body of Alfred Evans, discovered about four months later, near Smith's body, was not "linked." And there was Mrs. Williams's contention that there had been fourteen murders while her son was in jail.

And there may have been, indeed, fourteen, or forty, they were not to be reckoned with, unless they "fit the pattern." They had not, in fact, *happened* unless they "fit the pattern." And this relentlessly inscrutable Oriental "pattern" was the creation of D. A. Slaton, who, only yesterday, would have referred us to "police figures." "We knew," Slaton assured us, in measured tones, "when we arrested him that there would be no more [crimes that fit the pattern]. There have been no more."

Certainly not.

Then there was Wayne Williams, himself as big and intransigent and puny as life. In a sense, he was, apart from the fiber evidence (which can be considered man-made), God's gift to the Prosecution.

I am thankful not to have been on that jury. Someone described Wayne Williams's *karma*—for which I read *aura*—as terrifying. I would have described it as vindictive: *somebody*, as the old Sly and the Family Stone hit puts it, *you'd just love to burn.*

This is an awkward way to feel concerning someone on the witness stand. I have studied him only on television—but the human face can dissemble nothing before that particular camera, which is more probing than a doctor and far more ruthless than a mirror.

The boy seemed to me possessed by a blind, invalid arrogance, and every human being, as his eye flicked over or flinched against them, became, immediately, as malleable as his mother and his father. This is the reason, as I have said, that I really do not believe him guilty. He is far, far too indolent: I do not believe that, for him, other people are sufficiently real to elicit anything so dangerous as passion. Passion may be the province of nightmares, but it is far from the land of dreams.

Williams struck me as a spoiled, lost, and vindictive child, sheltered, somehow, from the storm of puberty, for whom others existed only as a means of proving his power to manipulate—which can be considered, after all, the story of his brief life.

(But, to be honest, this statement, which refers to his tyranny over his parents, immediately connects, for me, with an image of some of the children being stripped and bathed—as Wayne may have been, for far too long—before being murdered. It is conceivable that Wayne was compelled to make the doomed attempt to smother the child his parents smothered. A horrible thought, but this is a horrible case, and vengeance takes many forms.)

Some people argued that, if Wayne hadn't been such a smart-ass, he might never have come to trial at all. He wasn't arrested on the bridge, after all, and it might have been difficult to prove his presence on the bridge. He may have opened his big mouth once too often, when, in response to the question, "What were you doing on the bridge?," he answered, "I was on the bridge to get to the other side." Thus, we know now, from the testimony of this painfully condescending aristocrat, that he was on the bridge, as claimed.

The reasons he subsequently gives to explain his presence— that he was verifying the address of the phantom Johnson woman, with whom he had an appointment later that same morning—can strike one only as preposterous, or desperate: one thinks of the small boy, caught with his hands in the cookie jar, brazening, stone walling it out. Mrs. Williams insists that the Johnson woman was an FBI plant—that Wayne was deliberately lured to the bridge—but this is unconvincing, if only because Wayne does not claim to have had an *appointment* with anyone on the bridge at that or any hour.

But it seems to me almost equally improbable that he would select that hour and that place to dispose of the body. Bodies, as I have said, were being found all over Atlanta. It would seem to have been much safer, and simpler, to have driven a few miles and dumped the body in the weeds. And, if the river was chosen because the murderer had discovered the threat of fiber evidence, this still seems an odd moment and an unnecessarily public place. Though the river was being watched, no river can be watched along its entire length. The bridge was a stakeout—though this last detail may not have been known to Williams.

But none of this helps us to decide Wayne Williams innocent or guilty. There is speculation that Cater and Payne had to be killed because they had helped Wayne with the previous murders. This is a conceivable scenario, though it leaves begging the question why they didn't decide to kill *him*. But it is certainly conceivable that Wayne Williams, at some point, panicked, and decided to silence his accomplices. (If accomplices they were.) If he knew of the fiber evidence, he would certainly have gone to the river—fire, which would have done just as well, would, also, have posed too many hazards. This scenario would account for what can be read as the incoherent panic of his behavior.

This will remain, now, however, forever in the realm of speculation, there being nothing in life connecting Cater, Payne, and Williams, and, in death, nothing but an unlikely and untidy murder case—or, more precisely, an unlikely case and an untidy trial.

Untidy indeed, and, in performance, apparently, very often unpleasant. Mary Welcome, who is the lawyer chosen by Williams, brought with her Alvin Binder, a White lawyer, from Mississippi, and Tony Axam a Black lawyer, from Atlanta.

In show business, this trio would have bombed in the boondocks, far from the Broadway lights. Binder endeared himself to no one, particularly not the jury, by wondering if Lee Brown spoke the English language, or by calling Wayne Williams a "boy." He did not endear himself to Tony Axam, either, but Axam a sardonic, good-natured, self-contained man, who impressed me very much—he has, as the old folks say, "good sense"—had not expected Binder to be endearing. He had not expected Binder to be there at all. It was Mary Welcome's idea, not his, and no one appears to know what gave Mary Welcome this particular idea. As for Axam he had experience and skills as a trial lawyer that Mary Welcome lacked, and told him that she lacked.

And, here, we come upon another aspect of this case, an

aspect brutal and obvious, once one thinks about it, but one doesn't think about it before one is forced to think about it.

Wayne Williams is at the center of this drama, and pulling many of the strings, but his fate is not the only fate at issue. The Judge, for example, may possibly find himself in a no-win situation: the introduction of the prior-acts cases *can* be challenged. On the other hand, to have thwarted this introduction would have been so seriously to damage the Prosecution's case as to have virtually guaranteed defeat, and the Judge could, also, then, in principle, have been accused by the jury of withholding information. Yet further to compound the dilemma, someone who knows the law pointed out to me that "*the evidence was so incredibly favorable to the Prosecution as to be [legally] prejudicial.*"

The Law is not the only reality in a lawyer's life. Lawyers have rent to pay, status to achieve, or maintain, children to feed, and heights to scale. All this costs money, and costs much more than money. The key to the performance, or the value of the lawyer is to be found in what he takes as real. I was not being malicious when I mentioned the probable fate of this "trio" in show business. I was only suggesting that their divergences made it impossible for them to operate as a team.

Axam left first, to the great joy of the Prosecution. (Perhaps he will tell his story, on another day.) Then, Binder left, and, finally, Wayne Williams dismissed Mary Welcome, and/or she resigned, these actions occurring virtually simultaneously.

Mary Welcome is the adopted daughter of Verna Welcome, senator, from Maryland.

I met Verna Welcome, many years ago, in Montgomery, Alabama. On the steps of the federal courthouse, in fact, from which legal sanctuary, and under the American (as distinguished from the Confederate) flag, the Sheriff was forcibly removing us, despite the presence of the Justice Department, and the FBI. Neither of these representatives could do, as they plaintively informed me, "anything about it."

Mary Welcome could not go long unnoticed anywhere, and she did not go long unnoticed in Atlanta. She had been married to someone "from one of the islands," has a son, and came to Atlanta after she and her husband were divorced—in the early seventies, when she would have been very young. "She was warm," according to one of my informants, "outgoing. *Very* attractive." She became a part of the law firm Kennedy, Samson, and Edwards, and, then, was appointed city solicitor, a four-year appointment, during which time she tried misdemeanor cases and became something of a celebrity. At the end of this term, Jesse Hill, chairman of the board and president of the Atlanta Life Insurance Company, is instrumental, apparently, in her becoming part of the "preeminent" Mississippi law firm, Kennedy, Samson, Bussey, and Edwards, and, having won her spurs, she is, by 1980, in private practice.

She was on *Nightline*, she was on all the TV shows, and there was even a craze for "Mary Welcome shades" because Ms. Welcome wears (and, on her, they do not seem an affectation) enormous, square dark glasses. She was prominent in one of those clean-up-the-city campaigns, centering on bathhouses and prostitution, and achieved a kind of storm-center notoriety with her contradictory handling of two rape cases. In the first, a Black dance-hall girl accused a Black police officer of having forcibly sodomized her, and Ms. Welcome defended the girl, and won the case.

She also won the second case, in which three Morris Brown

students were accused of having gang-raped one lone Black girl, having dragged her, if my notes are accurate, to the empty gymnasium for this purpose. She was, in any case, raped, nor did the boys make any attempt to deny it; they seemed rather proud to be informed of the lacerating power of their tools. Prior acts figured very largely in this case, the prior acts being those of the girl, and proving that she was not (nor had she claimed to be) a virgin. Not only that, but one of her assailants swore that she had touched him "in the groin area" about a week before the gang rape, which made it difficult, presumably, to know what she was complaining about. (And someone quotes Ms. Welcome as saying, in court, "You want to condemn my client because he had sex with a bad girl!")

This is the lawyer Wayne Williams chose to defend him. I am told that Wayne Williams would probably have met her while she was city solicitor, and while Wayne was acting, in effect, as unofficial, unconnected (and apparently unwanted) police reporter. He was, I am told, in what was described to me as an "imitation" unmarked police car, and with his camera and tape-recording equipment, at the scene of every accident, every crime, even going so far as attempting to get a job in the morgue.

Ms. Welcome asked Axam to try the case with her, and he agreed. How Binder was decided upon is not clear, except, I am told, that "no White lawyer [from Atlanta] would have tried the case with her" and Welcome would, presumably, have known Binder from her season with the "preeminent" Mississippi law firm.

This is a disastrously mismatched trio, as Wayne Williams, dimly and ineffectually, seems to have begun to apprehend.

Axam for example, takes the position, essentially, that the

Prosecution *has* no case before it *proves* it has a case. Therefore, the Defense need not burden itself with *dis*proving what are, until evidence proves otherwise, mere allegations. The Defense, that is, is not so much compelled to prove Wayne *innocent* as the State is compelled to *prove* him guilty.

This cannot be done by following the Prosecution's lead, and asking witnesses, as Binder does, *Did he ever sexually molest you?* This irrelevant question simply confirms for the jury (and no matter how the question is answered) the idea of Wayne's depravity.

There was, also, an attempt, apparently, to prove that no crime had taken place. This was taken as a sign that the Defense was desperate. And the Defense spent thousands of dollars, apparently, to bring a pathologist from Jerusalem to prove that Cater and Payne had died natural deaths, while swimming, because they suffered from enlarged hearts. The jury was impressed, as I am, by this energy, but was not, unluckily, convinced, nor am I.

The charge against Wayne is not even addressed by attempting to compare him to a "dreamer," like Martin Luther King, Jr., whose relationship to the children he is alleged to have turned into corpses was that of big brother, prophet, and guide. No one, having taken one look at Wayne Williams, would dream of casting him in this role, and the argument reeks, moreover, of a kind of hypocritical, moral blackmail, which alienates, because it patronizes, the jurors, and, again, suggests that the Defense is on the ropes.

And it was disastrous for the Defense to claim, "There has never been a Black mass murderer," for it allowed Slaton to reply, unanswerably, *"Idi Amin was a Black mass murderer."*

Furthermore, it is worth pointing out that, according to

witnesses, crucial questions were answered beyond the hearing of the jury or the public, for the Judge, at those moments, requested the lawyers to approach the bench.

Finally, this tension and dissension had a terrible effect on Wayne Williams, who, shortly, did not know which lawyer to believe. And, though there were no other crimes that "fit the pattern," there were crimes enough. It could not have been difficult to convey to him that he, who had been "linked" to so many crimes, could yet be "linked" to others. I think that it was this panic that caused him to dismiss Tony Axam and, finally, Mary Welcome.

But, in the beginning, she must have seemed to him a swarthy, female F. Lee Bailey.

She may have thought of this, too; indeed, it would have been almost impossible for her not to have thought of this. For this exceedingly complex, notorious, and repellent affair is the kind of case, precisely, that can make or break a career. If Ms. Welcome was as convinced of Wayne's innocence as is, apparently, Wayne himself, then she would have had no choice but to help Wayne nourish his dream. He continued his projects, by mail, and tried to hold his record group together, by mail.

Mentally, Wayne is White, somebody told me, and I still don't quite know what to make of that statement. I suppose the statement refers to his dream of fame and dominance, and the rewards. Unluckily, in my experience, the only people capable of *dreaming* of fame and dominance are those mercilessly mediocre creatures who, sometimes, unluckily for us all, achieve a semblance of these. Unluckily, because to *dream* of fame and dominance is to dream in quotation marks and desire to transform oneself into a resounding and unanswerable quotation. Since pain and danger, however, accompany every journey, hope, and delusion, my informant may have been trying *not* to wonder if Wayne despised Black flesh enough to destroy it—which has been, indeed, the principal and unanswerable action of the White mentality; and this question, obviously, does not apply only to Wayne.

The Williams family disliked Ms. Welcome, and Ms. Williams refused to allow Ms. Welcome to examine her.

One of my informants tried to call Camille Bell, at the beginning of the Terror, and was unable to get through. She finally managed to speak to her, much later, not without difficulty, for, by this time, Ms. Bell had been forcibly upgraded to the status of an unlisted number.

The following exchange took place:

Ms. Bell: You're one of the few friends we have in the middle class. . . .
My informant: I haven't always been middle class. . . .
Ms. Bell: Well, *I* have!

I think I understand the meaning of this exceedingly laconic and loaded exchange, which could take place only among Black people, in this country, now.

I remember a boy named Buddy, just before or just after I joined the church. I was about fourteen. He was seventeen. I met him a few times, very briefly. He had been a friend of the "older" boys in church, but they no longer spoke to him.

I remember seeing him, for the last time, on the avenue, in the daytime. I was coming home from school. He looked very sad and weary, with a cigarette between his heavy lips.

I remember the cigarette because the cigarette signaled, proved, his sinful state. He had been a member of the church, sanctified, holy, but had "backslid," had "gone back into the world," and we were forbidden to speak to him. By speaking to Buddy, I risked a reprimand and might have been forced to undertake a purifying fast.

Yet, I spoke to him. We talked for a little while. But he scarcely knew me—I was not one of the "older" boys. I still remember his face, lightless and lonely, unbelievably lonely, looking at something far away or deep within.

I remember watching him walk away, down the avenue. In my memory, he is wearing a black winter coat. I never saw him again. Very shortly afterward, he died, I was told, of TB: tuberculosis.

The encounter, his face, and the aftermath—his death— haunted me for many years; in some way, obviously, it haunts me still. I had the feeling, dimly, then, but very vividly later, that he died because he had been rejected by the only commu- nity he knew, that we had had it in our power to bring the light back to his eyes. He was a sinner and he died, therefore, in sin; but, we are all sinners. *Let him who is without sin among you cast the first stone.* But I could not say that, then. It was when I found myself unable *not* to say it that I, too, left the church— the community; and it took me many years to realize that the community that had formed me had also brought about that hour and that rupture.

I was acting, after all, on the moral assumptions I had inherited from the community that had produced me. I had been told to *love everybody.* Whoever else did not believe this, *I* did. The way of the transgressor is hard, indeed, but it is hard because the community produces the transgressor in order to renew itself. I am afraid that this mathematic, this inexora- bility, will last as long as life lasts, and I would not have to risk sounding so grandiose were I not under the necessity of attempting to excavate the meaning of the word *community*—which, as I have understood it, simply means our endless connection with, and responsibility for, each other.

I say all that to suggest this: there is something profound and unanswerable stirring in the consciousness of all mankind today, and our identities, with every breath we take, are being altered. There is nothing anyone can do to halt or prevent this metamorphosis. And, if my memory of Buddy somehow triggers this apprehension, it has something to do with my sense that one is always doing one's first works over. The key to the presumed generality can be found only in the merciless particular. I have suggested that Buddy's rejection by the community helped bring about his death—left him no choice but death. This may seem an exaggerated statement, but I think that the exaggeration may be a useful one. For while there is no guarantee that the community could have, as a friend of mine puts it, "kissed the hurt away," his sense of being valued might have made the split-second difference between choosing life and choosing death. All of our lives really hang on some such tiny thread and it is very dangerous not to know this.

In any case, we are all born into communities, whether we like it or not or know it or not and whether or not we get along with the community. And, when I speak of *doing one's first works over*, I am referring to the movement of the human soul, in crisis, which, then, is forced to reexamine the depths from which it comes in order to strike water from the rock of the inheritance.

In the twentieth century, and in the modern State, the idea—the sense—of community has been submerged for a very long time. In the United States, the idea of community scarcely means anything anymore, as far as I can tell, except among the submerged, the "lowly": the Native American, the Mexican, the Puerto Rican, the Black. These can be called communities because they are informed by their knowledge that only they of the community can sustain and re-create each other. The great, vast, shining Republic knows nothing about them and cares nothing about them—recognizes their existence only in time of stress, as during a military adventure, say, or an election year, or when their dangerous situation erupts into what the Republic generally calls a "riot." And it goes without saying that these communities, incipient, wounded, or functioning, are between the carrot and the stick of the American Dream.

But the American Dream can be taken as the final manifestation of the European/Western/Christian dominance. There are no more oceans to cross, no savage territories to be conquered, no more natives to be converted. (And those for sale have been bought.) In a world made hideous by man-made poverty and obscenely senseless war, it is hard to predict the future of money: when the South African miner leaves the mines, what happens to the price of gold?

The present social and political apparatus cannot serve human need.

It is this apprehension that ferments in multitudes today, looking at the bodies of their menaced and uselessly slaughtered children, all over this world, in Atlanta, and from sea to shining sea. Do not misunderstand what I know can very easily be read merely as an accusation. I do not have the European (or provincial) liberty to write *J'Accuse*. (Think about it.) This is the only nation under heaven that contains the universe—east and west, north and south, black and white. This is the only nation in the world that can hope to liberate—to begin to liberate—mankind from the strangling idea of the national identity and the tyranny of the territorial dispute. I know this sounds remote, now, and that I will not live to see anything resembling this hope come to pass. Yet, I know that I *have* seen it—in fire and blood and anguish, true, but I have seen it. I speak with the authority of the issue of the slave born in the country once believed to be: *the last best hope of earth.*

Finally, it is perfectly possible that Wayne Williams must be added to the list of Atlanta's slaughtered black children. I do not think that the Black community, or, for that matter, the White one, can afford to ignore the moral dilemma as well as the moral opportunity posed by his incarceration.

The author of a crime is what he is—he knows it, can make no more demands, nor is anything more demanded of him. But he who collaborates is doomed, bound forever in that unimaginable and yet very common condition which we weakly suggest as *Hell.* In that condition, and every American walking should know it, one can never again summon breath to cry *let my people go!*

FOREWORD FROM THE TEN-YEAR

ANNIVERSARY EDITION

For all who appreciate a master's rendering of the written word, a new edition of any of James Baldwin's work is cause for celebration. In this reissue of his 1985 essay on the Atlanta child murders, *The Evidence of Things Not Seen*, Baldwin presents a painfully revealing portrait of a city's crisis. He lays bare the pervasive presence of race that moved so many to protect the image of the city rather than address the conditions that led to the deaths of many young black people.

Invited back into America's racial cauldron from his voluntary exile in France, Baldwin enlists fact and faith to try to make sense of what he refers to as a series of murders prosecuted as a mass murder. Applying the template of his own ambivalent and troubling history in America as a black child in a white country, he is able to convey a sense of how such an awful tragedy could happen in a city that had carefully crafted an image as the "city too busy to hate."

In his role of literary reporter, Baldwin eschews a search

for clues and, instead, undertakes an exploration for truths. Once engaged, he follows his own leads, relying on personal perception and a probing intellect. He asks questions that may be unanswerable, and he posits theories that are at once familiar to the African-American experience and frightening in their familiarity. And, in his unique style, he analyzes the effect of pervasive racism on the behavior of all the players in this tense, complex, and unsettling drama.

James Baldwin was not a lawyer, yet his commentary on the Atlanta trial is enlightened by his astute assumption that racism in American law cannot be understood by reading statutes and legal decisions removed from the context of the political, economic, and social concerns that gave rise to them. Utilizing his knowledge and the uncannily accurate insights for which he was famous, Baldwin produced a provocative and powerful work that continues to inform long after the events in Atlanta have been superseded by later and even scarier events.

In recalling the horror of the Atlanta murders—conditioned as we were to expect that racist police or a KKK-type group was responsible—it was deeply disturbing when a young black man, Wayne Williams, was prosecuted and convicted of the crimes. Our and Baldwin's unease was heightened by the knowledge that Williams seemed more indolent than energetic and that his parents and those who knew him viewed him as spoiled, arrogant, and something of a failure. Williams was not the racist specter we expected, but young black men his age—and far younger—are becoming, ready or not, the specters our society is spawning in ever-increasing numbers.

Our suspicions of a decade ago have been replaced by a weary resignation. Poet Maya Angelou expresses the plight of our most deprived with great poignancy when she writes:

In these bloody days and frightful nights when an urban warrior can find no face more despicable than his own, no ammunition more deadly than self-hate and no target more deserving of his true aim than his brother, we must wonder how we came so late and lonely to this place.*

Reading Baldwin's ruminations on Atlanta a decade later, we can recognize that he provided us with fearful prophesies about today's worsening life chances for those born poor and black. Deeply embedded racial beliefs and presumptions doomed the Atlanta children to an environment where all manner of predicaments and perils haunted their days and threatened their lives. Now, those dangers have grown worse in a volatile economic climate in which politicians posture about solutions and settle for scapegoats.

For politicians, "fear of crime" becomes both a readily translatable code for anti-black rhetoric and a convenient cover for the serious domestic issues that they prefer to ignore and for which they present no real solutions. For example, debate over the morality—to say nothing of the deterrent value—of the death penalty is subsumed under the unseemly competition to apply it to more and more crimes. Application of the ultimate penalty, it is assumed without acknowledgment or shame, will condemn a disproportionately large number of blacks.

Where execution is not available, imprisonment has become the social policy of choice. Again, blacks will bear the brunt of politically popular alternatives to addressing seriously the disappearance of jobs. In 1993, 53 percent of black males in the

---

* Maya Angelou, "I Dare to Hope," *New York Times*, August 25, 1991, p. 15.

prime working and family-forming years—the ages of twenty-five to thirty-four—were jobless or employed with wages too low to raise a family of four out of poverty. As a direct result of the closing off of access to legal employment, 80 to 85 percent of black men in urban areas will be caught up in the criminal "justice" system, most on drug-related charges, before they reach their thirtieth birthday—if they are lucky enough to live that long. The number of black men in prison now exceeds 800,000, the largest number of any country in the world. That number is expected to reach one million before the year 2000.

Because our society does not view itself in any way responsible for antisocial deviance by blacks that leads to their deaths or incarceration, black crime statistics with all their unhappy ramifications are treated not as a serious political and social problem, but as a challenge to the nation's commitment to law and order. In the face of massive evidence that it will do little to reduce either the fear or the fact of crime, the Street Crime Act of 1994 provides billions of dollars for new prisons and creates new categories of crime that ensure our ever-growing penal system will be filled with those whom society abandons and betrays.

It is not difficult to believe that Baldwin's skepticism about virtually every aspect of the Atlanta case is founded in his recognition that as horrible as were the facts of that case, the criminalizing of social problems would become much worse without any reasonable possibility that, at some point, we would see the light. Baldwin maintains that his "soul is a witness," and the Atlanta case has transcended its time without shedding light as to whether we fail to halt the devastation of black people because we—as a society—are unable to or because we do not want to.

Of course, clairvoyance is not required to predict with certainty how America would have responded in Atlanta had the victims been white boys from "good" homes, the suspects all black, and the murders apparently racially motivated. Similarly, if mainly white suburbs were experiencing the strife that has turned inner-city neighborhoods into battlegrounds, the crisis response would recognize the danger to all that, in fact, exists.

Baldwin, though, doubts whether even tardy recognition that the danger and destruction is not limited to black ghettoes would be sufficient to move America to reconcile the clear need for emergency action with the country's racial pathologies. He writes: "For the action of the White Republic, in the lives of Black men, has been, and remains, emasculation. Hence, the Republic has absolutely no image, or standard, of masculinity to which any man, Black or White, can honorably aspire." Reluctant even to try and imagine what whites see when they look at blacks, he knows that "whatever this vision, or nightmare, is, it corrodes the life of the Republic on every level."

The magic and virtue of Baldwin's pen is that it rings with what one knows instinctively and from a great depth is truth. There are, of course, harsh challenges and no promise of survival, to say nothing of victory, in that truth. Baldwin's faith, like that of Paul and the other biblical prophets he so loved to quote, "is the substance of things hoped for, the evidence of things not seen."

It is thus as prophet urging us on—not as doomsayer—that he defines the terms of black existence in this country, warning:

> It is a very grave matter to be forced to imitate a people for whom you know—which is the price of your performance and survival—you do not exist. It is hard to imitate a people

whose existence appears, mainly, to be made tolerable by their bottomless gratitude that they are not, thank heaven, *you.*

There is in this work—as there is in so much of Baldwin's literary legacy—a finely balanced cry of despair and a quiet prayer of wonderment. Illustrative of this reflection on a people's ordeal and salvation, he writes:

A stranger to this planet might find the fact that there are any Black people at all still alive in America something to write home about. I, myself find it remarkable not that so many Black men were forced (and in so many ways!) to leave their families, but that so many remained and aided their issue to grow and flourish.

Baldwin's work cries out against the contradictions, the delusions—the manipulation of power—while he searches for that elusive love that would illuminate our moral obligation and, therefore, salvage our fragile civilization.

—DERRICK BELL WITH JANET DEWART BELL
October 1994

ABOUT THE AUTHOR

James Baldwin's celebrated works of fiction include *Go Tell It on the Mountain, Giovanni's Room, Another Century, Tell Me How Long the Train's Been Gone, If Beale Street Could Talk, Just Above My Head*, and the short story collection *Going to Meet the Man*. He was also the author of a book of poetry, *Jimmy's Blues*, two dramatic works, *Blues for Mister Charlie* and *The Amen Corner*, and many works of nonfiction, including *Nobody Knows My Name, The Fire Next Time*, and *Notes of a Native Son*. Born in Harlem in 1924, he lived for many years in France, where he died in 1987.